T0282120

THE CLASSICAL WORLD

IN BITE-SIZED CHUNKS

Also by Mark Daniels

World Mythology in Bite-sized Chunks
Gods, Heroes and Monsters

THE CLASSICAL WORLD

IN BITE-SIZED CHUNKS

MARK DANIELS

Michael O'Mara Books Limited

First published in Great Britain in 2024 by
Michael O'Mara Books Limited
9 Lion Yard
Tremadoc Road
London SW4 7NQ

A CIP catalogue record for this book is available from the British Library.

This product is made of material from well-managed, FSC®-certified
forests and other controlled sources. The manufacturing processes
conform to the environmental regulations of the country of origin.

ISBN: 978-1-78929-655-6 in hardback print format
ISBN: 978-1-78929-714-0 in trade paperback format
ISBN: 978-1-78929-657-0 in ebook format

1 2 3 4 5 6 7 8 9 10

Cover illustrations by Jessica Benhar
Jacket design by Natasha Le Coultre
Designed and typeset by D23

Printed and bound by CPI Group (UK) Ltd, Croydon, CR0 4YY
www.mombooks.com

MIX
Paper | Supporting
responsible forestry
FSC
www.fsc.org
FSC® C171272

CONTENTS

INTRODUCTION

I was never very good at history when I was at school. The lessons felt like a series of memory tests to me, in which we had to remember whether a certain king came to power in AD 1189 or AD 1199. It was all dates and no substance, as far as a bored twelve-year-old schoolboy could work out. It wasn't until I discovered Classics that the dust blew off those historical documents, and real, human life emerged from the pages. Because the classical world isn't just a spot of history. Of course, it includes the history of the Ancient Greeks and the Ancient Romans, but it is so much more than that. There exists such a rich and unrivalled abundance of literature, mythology, architecture, language, customs and art that has remained from both Greece and Rome, that the civilizations themselves become living, breathing experiences that we can feel as keenly today as their citizens did thousands of years ago.

You can't walk around the Colosseum in Rome without hearing the roar of 80,000 spectators baying for blood. You can't watch the Greek tragedies of Aeschylus without feeling the same gut-wrenching pain his audiences felt in 458 BC. You can't read the philosophical musings of Socrates without questioning what it means to be human, even today. Suddenly, these ancient civilizations don't feel very ancient at all.

When you wander into the lives of the Ancient Greeks and Romans, you discover their life-affirming lessons of philosophy, you cry, gasp and shudder at their poetry, and you gaze in utter disbelief at their architecture that has not yet been bettered. (The largest unsupported concrete dome in the world is still one that was built nearly two thousand years ago for Rome's Pantheon. We're still trying to work out how they built it.)

In mythology, they have given us heroic Hercules, snake-haired Medusa, the one-eyed Cyclops and the deceptive Trojan Horse. In language, English uses words directly from Greek such as *catastrophe*, *drama* and *xenophobe*, and from Latin such as *ad hoc*, *P.S.* and *vice versa*. Our system of democracy, how we run our courts, and how we build our concert arenas are all influenced by the classical world. There would be no *Romeo and Juliet* without Ovid's original lovers, Pyramus and Thisbe. There would be no *Harry Potter* without the ancient heroes' journeys undertaken by Odysseus and Aeneas. The brains of the classical world have given us Pythagoras' theorem, they proved the world was round 1,700 years before Columbus set foot on a boat, and – unbelievably – they even invented automatic doors.

Imagine a world without concrete. A world without paved roads. A world without flushing toilets. A world without warm baths. A world without pizza. They haven't just influenced modern society and culture, they have shaped it entirely.

So, throw away your dusty old history books, and

instead enter into the living and breathing soul of a world that feels remarkably familiar. Hear how the Greeks and Romans loved, laughed and cried. Be amazed by their technology and towering structures, read some of the oldest stories ever told, and wonder at how much of the globe these ancient civilizations wandered over.

In 101 delightfully snackable bite-sized chunks, step into your own experience of the amazing Classical World.

CHAPTER 1

THE GODS

Introduction
to the Pantheon

The pantheon of gods and goddesses in Greek and Roman mythology is a seemingly endless list of deities, demigods, nymphs, spirits and guides. They can be vengeful or supportive; they can start wars or halt them; and they can raise up huge storms or calm them. They have the power to take on any form they choose; they can make a hero stand tall in battle; or they can sow discord and fear in an army of soldiers.

They rule the skies, the seas and the afterlife, and it is the gods' actions and decisions that influence everything that happens in the mortal world. When the gods argue, humankind goes to war; when they celebrate, mortals fall in love; when they mourn, there is famine on Earth. And with enough love, jealousy and fights between the gods to rival any reality TV show, there is no end of upheaval, drama and chaos for us mere mortals.

Pantheons of gods and goddesses have been used in many ancient civilizations – from the Mayans to the Māoris – to try to make sense of the inexplicable and the unpredictable in life. Across the globe, civilizations that had no contact with one another have created a remarkably similar character list of gods, who create and control the world in similar ways. Entirely unrelated mythologies have a sky father and a mother Earth, a male Sun and female Moon, a god of chaos and one bringing order. One god is responsible for the creation of humankind, often moulded from clay or mud, and gives us clothes, the ability to make fire, and teaches us laws, morals and commandments. It is easier to explain death, famine, storms, the Sun and love through the narrative of powerful gods than it is to try to make sense of those things in any other way.

The gods of the classical world are far from perfect. They are prone to mistakes, deceit and envy. And they don't seem to have the power to protect humans from the one guiding force that we must all face: our fate. If a terrible prophecy has been made in Greek tragedy, or a mythological hero has been given his powerful destiny to fulfil, the gods often play against one another with delaying tactics. But the ultimate fate of the mortal protagonist always catches up with them.

Greek mythology predates Roman mythology by up to a thousand years, and the Greeks really were at their most powerful and influential from the fourth and fifth centuries BC, versus the Romans' global influence that properly got going from the first century BC. What that means is that Greek legends, architecture and mythology felt like something very ancient and grand to the Romans of Augustus Caesar's reign. The Parthenon in the centre of Athens would have been a 400-year-old monument in the eyes of the Roman architects who created the Pantheon building in the centre of Rome. When the Romans designed buildings with huge columns and porticos, they were

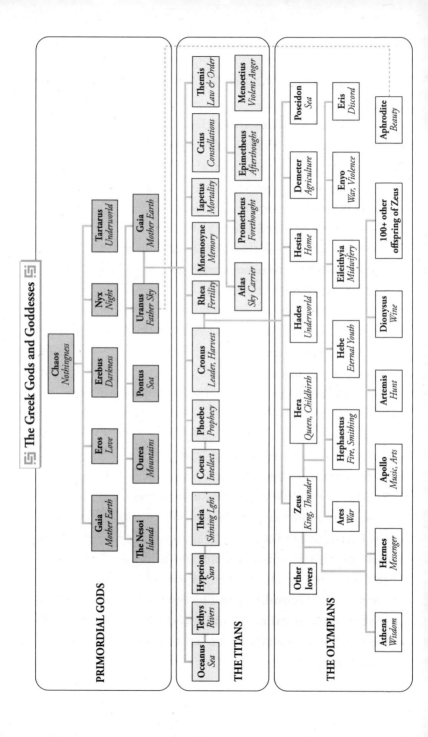

The Greek Gods and Goddesses

PRIMORDIAL GODS

Chaos *Nothingness*

Gaia *Mother Earth*
Eros *Love*
Erebus *Darkness*
Nyx *Night*
Tartarus *Underworld*
Gaia *Mother Earth*

The Nesoi *Islands*
Ourea *Mountains*
Pontus *Sea*
Uranus *Father Sky*

THE TITANS

Oceanus *Sea*
Tethys *Rivers*
Hyperion *Sun*
Theia *Shining Light*
Coeus *Intellect*
Phoebe *Prophecy*
Cronus *Leader, Harvest*
Rhea *Fertility*
Mnemosyne *Memory*
Iapetus *Mortality*
Crius *Constellations*
Themis *Law & Order*

Atlas *Sky Carrier*
Prometheus *Forethought*
Epimetheus *Afterthought*
Menoetius *Violent Anger*

THE OLYMPIANS

Athena *Wisdom*
Other lovers
Hermes *Messenger*
Zeus *King, Thunder*
Ares *War*
Hera *Queen, Childbirth*
Apollo *Music, Arts*
Hephaestus *Fire, Smithing*
Hestia *Home*
Hades *Underworld*
Hebe *Eternal Youth*
Demeter *Agriculture*
Eileithyia *Midwifery*
Poseidon *Sea*

Artemis *Hunt*
Dionysus *Wine*
Enyo *War, Violence*
100+ other offspring of Zeus
Eris *Discord*

Aphrodite *Beauty*

borrowing centuries of Greek grandeur and excellence, and claiming it as their own.

The Romans did exactly the same with the gods of Greek mythology. They took these ancient deities and myths, gave them all Roman names, and continued to embellish the stories about them. Greek Zeus became Roman Jupiter; Greek Aphrodite became Roman Venus; and Greek Ares became Roman Mars. The two religions aren't exactly the same: the older Greek theology is more likely to give names and personalities to phenomena such as Discord, Rumour and Love, whereas the Roman gods are generally more human in form. But in effect, the main characters of both pantheons are treated as the same gods and goddesses.

Some deities were simply given more Roman-sounding names, while others were merged with existing Roman gods – the distinctly Greek Athena being mapped onto the existing Roman goddess Minerva. Throughout this book, I have used the Greek names for the gods, except where the stories or histories are uniquely Roman.

The pantheon of gods falls into three distinct generations. The Primordial Gods are the very earliest powers that brought the universe into existence, including Chaos and the Earth mother Gaia. The Titans are the next generation that got things going, including the original father of the sky, Cronus. Finally, the Olympians are the famous ones: Zeus, Aphrodite and Poseidon are all part of the generation that called Mount Olympus their home, and who inspired so many of the legends in both Greek and Roman mythology.

THE PRIMORDIAL GODS

Chaos

In the beginning, there is nothing. Chaos is the earliest stage of existence in the primordial universe, and is anthropomorphized as a female deity by early Greek religion. As later characters are introduced into the pantheon and the mythology becomes more sophisticated, Roman writers refer to Chaos as more of an amorphous mass of nonexistence before the universe came into being.

These primordial gods are as much deities as they are places, founding concepts and emotions. Their existence in humankind's mythology seems to predate the lively and complicated characters that make up the pantheon we know from much of Greek and Roman literature. What little is written about them changes and is contradictory, and they possess less characterization and humanity than the generations that are added later.

From Chaos come five gods. First to rise up is the Earth mother Gaia, then the deep underworld of Tartarus, followed by Eros, the personification of Love. It feels remarkable that one of the founding elements of the universe is Love, and yet it is what is needed for the other primordial gods to produce the rest of existence. Finally, both Erebus and Nyx – Darkness and Night respectively – are born from Chaos.

What is utterly staggering about the universe's formation out of Chaos is how similar it is to creation stories from civilizations the world over. Many mythologies that had no contact with one another tell of the world coming into being in a remarkably similar sequence. In the beginning, the world is in a dark, chaotic void with no life. The sky and the Earth separate, and the very first light shines between them. From there, the barren land is filled with rivers, lakes and vast oceans, which in turn bring grass, trees and fruit. Next come the animals and beasts, and finally humanity is given life.

The exact details vary between civilizations, but the same general sequence of events can be seen in the creation myths of the Ancient Egyptians in 3000 BC, of the Ancient Greeks as early as 1800 BC, of the Jewish and Christian Book of Genesis from about 500 BC, of the Incas in Peru in the thirteenth century AD, of the Māori people in New Zealand also in the thirteenth century AD, of the Sioux people of North America around AD 1300, and several others besides.

Gaia – Tellus Mater

The Greek goddess Gaia is known as Tellus Mater in Roman mythology – literally the Mother Earth. Her Greek name simply means Earth, and is the same root of the word *geography* ('study of earth') and the name *George* (meaning 'earth worker', or 'farmer'). Soon after coming into existence, Gaia creates her male counterpart, Uranus (the sky), the Nesoi ('the islands'), Ourea ('the mountains') and Pontus ('the sea'). She is the source of all life and, alongside Demeter, is worshipped to provide fertile land and bountiful food for her devotees.

Gaia's most notable role in classical mythology is her union with the sky god Uranus. Together, they rule over the world and they produce the next generation of gods: the mighty Titans. Early on in classical theology, the gods already start to display human traits of jealousy, fear and revenge that spans generations. Uranus worries that one of the Titans – his own children – will overthrow him, and it is matriarch Gaia who helps their son Cronus to do exactly that. After Cronus steps up to rule the skies, he has precisely the same anxiety over losing power to one of his own children – the Olympians. And once again, it is Gaia that helps her grandson, the heroic Olympian Zeus, to overthrow Cronus.

After Zeus takes control of the heavens and earth, Gaia even turns against him. She sends one of her offspring, the terrifying monster Typhon, into a colossal battle with Zeus. The seas crash, the earth shatters and Zeus' deafening thunderbolts see him victorious over the hundred-snake-headed beast. Unsatisfied, Gaia sends in her next brood – the immensely strong and arrogant Giants – to battle Zeus and overthrow all of the Olympian gods. A massive war breaks out, and the Olympians once again cement their role as rulers of the world.

Uranus – Caelus

As one of the primordial gods, Uranus is as much a representation of the skies and heavens as he is a deity. He is Gaia's equal and counterpart; she is the earth and he is the sky. He rarely appears in classical art and was not worshipped in his own right as many of the others were. Romans sometimes referred to him with the Greek name *Uranus*, but also mapped him onto existing deities representing the sky: calling him either Caelus or Aether.

As a ruler, Uranus is cruel and suspicious. In their union, he and Gaia produce the twelve Titan gods, the one-eyed Cyclopes monsters, and the fifty-headed, one-hundred-handed Hecatoncheires. Terrified that his position of power will be challenged, Uranus hates his children. As soon as each one is born, he hides them deep in the dark underworld of Tartarus, otherwise interpreted as pushing them back into Gaia's womb. She groans in agony and pleads with her children to punish Uranus' crimes. All of them are too scared to take on the task, except for one: the Titan god Cronus.

Gaia gives Cronus a shimmering, jagged-toothed sickle carved from flint rock, and he lies in ambush. Uranus approaches Gaia, ready to make love with her. As he lies down with her, Cronus flies forward, grabs his father's testicles with one hand and lifts the mighty sickle high above his head with the other. With one swift strike, he cuts off his father's testicles and throws them to the ground in victory. But the blood seeps into the earth – into Gaia – and she gives birth to the vengeful Furies, the arrogant

Giants and various nymphs. Cronus hurls Uranus' testicles into the frothing, white sea, from which emerges the goddess of beauty and lust, Aphrodite.

Her Greek name was believed to mean 'risen from froth', and a version of her birth out of a large scallop shell is captured in Botticelli's Renaissance painting *The Birth of Venus*, called after Aphrodite's Roman name.

This marks the end of Uranus' reign and indeed the end of his role in classical mythology. Cronus takes on the mantle as ruler of the skies, carrying the heavy warning from both Gaia and Uranus that he will bear a son, who will likewise challenge his powerful position.

Eros – Cupid

The Greek name Eros simply means *Love*. It is one of the primordial forces that is needed for Gaia and Uranus to produce all the gods and life that follows. However, as love is such an enduring and passionate emotion, the role of the god that represents it changes over time. Eros starts as this founding concept to kick-start the universe, but in later mythology is personified as a beautiful young god, whose arrows fly from a golden bow and move the most rational person into a love-mad frenzy. He is playful, mischievous and powerful enough to make even Zeus fall in love. In his evolution, later writers have Eros as the son of Aphrodite, rather than being a primordial god. She is the goddess of beauty and lust, and he is the god of love and desire.

Greek and Roman depictions start to make the handsome god even younger and even cuter, turning him into the cheeky, chubby cherub we're more familiar with.

It was Renaissance artists in the fourteenth century AD who cemented the imagery of Cupid, which endures on Valentine's Day cards today alongside romantic, arrow-speared hearts that he has pierced. Today, we talk of being 'love-struck' in honour of Eros' potent arrows.

Even Eros is not immune from the powers of love. His mother, Aphrodite, becomes jealous of a mortal woman named Psyche ('Soul'), whose beauty is so extraordinary that it is distracting people from properly worshipping the goddess of beauty herself. Aphrodite instructs Eros to pierce Psyche with the sweet wound of his arrow, to make her fall in love with the most miserable and hideous man on Earth.

But the love god is love-struck himself when he sees Psyche's unrivalled beauty. He abducts her away to his vast and luxurious palace as his wife, but hides his true identity. Only visiting her at night in the dark, he pleads with her not to look at his face. Psyche's wicked sisters become jealous of her new wealth, and they convince her to light a lantern and reveal her husband's identity while he is sleeping. She first spies his shimmering golden bow, then examines the strange arrows in his quiver. Running

Eros, the god of love.

her hand over them, one arrow pricks her finger; she falls even more deeply in love with her mysterious husband. Finally, looking at his face, she is so overcome with desire and love that she lets a drop of hot oil drip from the lantern she is holding, and she scalds the sleeping god. The trust is broken, and Eros leaves his wife.

On discovering the secret affair, Aphrodite rounds on the young Psyche and forces her to carry out a series of harsh labours. Eros discovers his lover overcome by one of these quests, and carries her up to Zeus on Mount Olympus. There, she is granted immortality so that the two may formally marry as equals, and put an end to the feud with Aphrodite.

THE TITANS

Cronus – Saturn

The Titans are twelve siblings, the second generation of gods, born from Gaia and Uranus. The most powerful of them is Cronus, who overthrows his father by castrating him with a sickle, taking over as the ruler of the heavens. This act of violence against his father is why Cronus is often depicted in ancient artwork and sculpture wielding the sickle or scythe that became his symbolic weapon. Despite their different origins, Cronus was frequently conflated with Chronos (the god of time), even in the ancient world, due to the similarity of their names. As a result, the enduring

A seventeenth-century painting by Giovanni Romanelli of Cronus abducting one of his children.

imagery of Father Time to this day shows him carrying a scythe – a tool originally associated with Cronus' castration of Uranus, rather than having anything to do with the concept of time itself. The grim reaper's archetypal scythe is a continuation of this misplaced iconography.

As Cronus usurped his father, it is no surprise that he himself should be suspicious of his own children. In fact, Gaia and Uranus warn their son that he will in turn be overthrown by a powerful heir. Cronus marries his sister, Rhea, and they produce six children – the third generation of gods known as the Olympians. This is where some of the more well-known characters start entering the scene: their children are Poseidon (god of the seas), Hades (god of the Underworld), Demeter (goddess of harvest), Hestia (goddess of the home), Hera (future queen of the heavens) and Zeus (future king of the heavens).

Taking a leaf out of Uranus' book on fatherhood, Cronus decides he has to dispatch each child as it is born. As Rhea gives birth to this new generation, Cronus takes each child and swallows them whole. He would have done away with all six of them, had Rhea not replaced the youngest boy – Zeus – with a rock wrapped in a blanket. Zeus is raised on the island of Crete in secret to become a powerful god.

In the first of Zeus' many shapeshifting shenanigans, as a young man he disguises himself as Cronus' cupbearer and gives him a vomit-inducing concoction. Zeus' fully grown siblings are all regurgitated, and they unite in an immense ten-year war known as the Titanomachy ('War of the Titans'), to decide who will rule the heavens: the Titans or the Olympians. Zeus and his siblings are victorious, heralding the new age of the Olympians, while the Titans are banished to Tartarus in the Underworld.

Roman mythology says that Saturn – the Roman version of Cronus – came to their land after banishment. He was widely celebrated in the origins of Rome, and was the focus of the most important festival in the Roman calendar: the Saturnalia.

The Saturnalia was a seven-day celebration of Saturn. It was held every December, with plants and candles brought into the home, presents given to children and charity to the poor. It had a direct influence on how Christmas is celebrated to this day.

Atlas

Atlas is the son of Iapetus, who is one of the original twelve Titans born to Gaia and Uranus. In the great ten-year Titanomachy war, in which Zeus and the Olympian gods fight to take power away from Cronus and the Titans, Atlas picks the wrong side. His brothers Prometheus and Epimetheus fight for the victorious Zeus, whereas Atlas and his other brother Menoetius side with the Titans. His punishment from the victor Zeus is to be banished to the extremities of the world, where he must hold up the heavens on his back for eternity.

Atlas in front of the Rockefeller Center in New York City.

Atlas is often pictured holding up the globe of the Earth on his back, and it is for this reason that an atlas (a collection of maps) is named after him. But the original myths have him holding up the celestial realm – rather than the earthly realm – for the rest of time. He gives his name to the Atlas Mountains, as well as to the Atlantic Ocean and to the fictional lost island of Atlantis.

One of Atlas' chances to escape from his position holding up the heavens comes when he meets Hercules. This archetypal Greek hero is a son of Zeus, following an affair with Alcmene. Zeus' wife Hera understandably hates Hercules' very existence, so drives him into a mad frenzy, during which he kills his wife and children. In atonement for the crimes, Hercules is sentenced to carry out twelve seemingly impossible quests. One of those Twelve Labours of Hercules is to grab some golden apples from three nymphs known as the Hesperides. Knowing that Atlas is the father of the Hesperides, Hercules realizes this could be his route to stealing the shimmering apples. He grants Atlas a brief respite from his eternal punishment by offering to hold up the heavens for him, in exchange for some golden apples from Atlas' daughters. Atlas willingly agrees, and sets the heavens onto Hercules' shoulders.

Everything seems to go well until Atlas returns with the apples. Unsurprisingly, the Titan decides he's had enough of holding up the entire heavens, and declares that Hercules can stick at the job himself. Without missing a beat, Hercules agrees – and just asks Atlas to relieve him for one moment so that he can make his cloak more comfortable. At which point, Hercules makes an inevitable dash, golden apples in hand.

Prometheus

When Gaia and Uranus produced the twelve original Titans, one of them – Iapetus – fathered Prometheus and Epimetheus, alongside Atlas. These two brothers became part of Zeus' inner circle after the Titanomachy war declared him the victorious ruler of the heavens. Prometheus' role in mythology changes over time, with earlier Greek writing having him as a god sympathetic towards humankind, while later Roman writing positions him as the creator of humans in the first place.

When the Earth was recently formed, it contained a divine power within it. Prometheus takes some of this new earth and mixes it with streams to form clay, from which the first humans are moulded. (It is curious that the Mayans – separated by oceans and millennia – had a similar myth for the first humans.) The Olympian gods hold a huge banquet to cement their relationship with humankind, and Prometheus presents two sacrificial offerings to Zeus. But he tries to trick the new ruler of the heavens: one offering has the best cuts of meat from the sacrificed bull, but they are hidden underneath unappetizing entrails; the other offering contains just bones, which have been disguised with more appealing white fat on top of them. Zeus accepts the second option, which gave Greek citizens their acceptable mythology as to why they kept the nicer bits of meat for themselves following a sacrifice to the gods.

Zeus is outraged at Prometheus for tricking him and punishes humanity by taking away from them the ability to make fire. But Prometheus later steals flames from the gods and takes them back to the mortals, teaching them how to harness the power of fire. The angered Zeus punishes humans by releasing evil spirits upon them through Pandora's box.

Prometheus' punishment is more gruesome still: he is chained to a rock where an eagle comes to pluck away his liver. Each day, his liver regrows and he must relive the agony again and again for eternity.

The Muses

The Titan goddess Mnemosyne, sister of Cronus and Rhea, is the personification of memory. Her name comes from a

Greek word for 'mindful', which is perpetuated in English words like 'mnemonic'. She is also the mother of the Muses, the nine sisters who inspire all the arts. This comes about because she sleeps with Zeus on nine consecutive nights, and as a result gives birth to nine daughters.

Many of the great pieces of Greek and Roman literature open with an invocation to the Muses to inspire the poet in his or her telling of a particular myth. The concept of writers and artists being inspired by Muses continued in Western art and literature for many centuries.

MUSE	AREA OF INSPIRATION	OFTEN SEEN CARRYING
Calliope	Muse of Epic Poetry	a writing tablet
Clio	Muse of History	scrolls
Erato	Muse of Lyric Poetry	a cithara (a string instrument)
Euterpe	Muse of Music	a flute-like instrument
Melpomene	Muse of Tragedy	a tragic mask
Polyhymnia	Muse of Hymns	a veil
Terpsichore	Muse of Light Verse and Dance	a lyre
Thalia	Muse of Comedy	a comic mask
Urania	Muse of Astronomy	a globe or compass

Even today, fashion designers speak of having a muse in one particular model or celebrity, whose body shape, personality or style they will use as inspiration in their development of new designs.

THE OLYMPIANS

Zeus – Jupiter

The Olympian gods officially refers to all of the deities who call Mount Olympus their home, but is often used to refer to just twelve of the key players, including Zeus and his most famous siblings and children. Sitting high on Mount Olympus, Zeus is in charge of the whole clan and is arbitrator of what is right or wrong. The gods come to him for the final say in difficult disputes, and he makes it very well known if you've displeased him in any way. One of his trademark lightning bolts would make his position very clear indeed. He is usually depicted wielding this weapon, and often with an eagle by his side or carrying his invincible shield, the aegis.

Many pantheons around the world feature a sky father figure. When the Romans adopted and adapted the Greek religion, they transposed Zeus into their own pantheon. The Roman name *Jupiter* derives from *Zeus-pater*, meaning 'Father Zeus'. The name Jove is another Latin version of the same word. Essentially, the names Zeus, Jupiter and Jove are not just representations of the same deity; they are the very same word that has undergone linguistic evolution and inflection, resulting in three different names. The Latin word *deus* ('god') and the English word 'divine' are all from the same root as *Zeus* and *Jupiter*.

Although Zeus is married to Hera, classical mythology is bursting to the seams with tales of his other lovers and children. With Hera, he fathers Ares (god of war) and Hephaestus (god of fire), alongside lesser-known Hebe (goddess of youth), Eileithyia (goddess of childbirth), Enyo (goddess of war) and Eris (goddess of discord). With other lovers, he fathers Athena (goddess of wisdom), Hermes (the messenger god), Apollo (god of music), Artemis (goddess of hunting) and Dionysus (god of wine). The rich legends of Greece and Rome put his final tally of children at over 110, which makes Hera's sometimes vengeful personality easy to sympathize with.

One of his many love affairs is with Europa, the beautiful princess of Phoenicia in modern-day Lebanon. Zeus is so enamoured by her that he morphs into a majestic white bull in order to seduce her. When Europa is picking flowers in a field with her friends, she spots the gleaming and powerful animal approaching her. The bull lowers its mighty head in submission, and astonished by its beauty, Europa climbs onto its back. Zeus walks the princess around the meadows, but then gathers pace, gallops away and dives into the sea with the screaming princess clinging on. Her grieving brother Cadmus travels the Earth in search of her, but never discovers that she has been hidden away on Crete. On that island, she gives birth to two legendary kings of the island, King Minos and King Rhadamanthys.

The name *Europa* for the geographical continent is given as early as the sixth century BC, if not even earlier, showing how impactful this legend of Zeus and his lover was.

Hera – Juno

Hera is the queen of the heavens and has a powerful role at Zeus' side on Mount Olympus. She is strong-willed, clever and holds authority among the gods. She is the goddess of marriage and motherhood, and a figure of protection for cities and young warriors. Her biggest impact in Greek and Roman mythology comes as a jealous wife and through her vengeful acts against the children of Zeus' more than one hundred documented affairs. She is instrumental in sparking the Trojan War; she is responsible for Hercules being given his twelve impossible labours; and she delays Roman hero Aeneas at almost every step towards founding the famous city of Rome.

One of Hera's many acts of revenge comes when she catches Zeus in the act of sleeping with the beautiful princess and nymph Io from Argos. In his haste to conceal yet another affair from his enraged wife, Zeus quickly turns Io into a beautiful white cow. Unconvinced by this deception, Hera demands the animal as a gift, and the bewildered princess is handed over. Under the gaze of Hera's appointed guard, the hundred-eyed giant Argus Panoptes, bovine Io cannot sleep with Zeus again.

Zeus comes up with a plan to free his lover: he sends the messenger god Hermes to distract the keen eyes of Argus Panoptes. Hermes lulls the giant to sleep with a song and is eventually able to kill him. With Hera's watchman defeated, Zeus sets Io free, but her ordeal is far from over. Hera sets a relentless gadfly to pursue and torment Io – still in her bovine form – across Europe and Asia, driving her ever onward in a desperate attempt to escape the maddening stings and bites. Io's journey takes her across the whole of Greece until she reaches the narrow strait separating Europe and Asia – the Bosphorus, a name that literally means 'ox ford', in honour of Io's journey across it. Finally, she settles down in Egypt, where Zeus can happily turn her back into human form.

Hades – Pluto

When Zeus and his brothers Hades and Poseidon are victorious in the Titanomachy battle between the old gods and the new generation, they draw lots to decide which of them will rule over which domain. Zeus becomes ruler of the skies, Poseidon becomes ruler of the seas, and Hades becomes ruler of the dark, murky Underworld. As such, Hades doesn't live on Mount Olympus and therefore can't officially be classed as an Olympian. But he's the brother of Zeus' generation, and is a key player in the mythology that surrounds the Olympians, and so I will include him in this chapter.

Hades is also the name given to the Underworld itself. It is the one place that all people go after they die, but where precisely within Hades you end up will dictate how enjoyable or painful your eternity in the afterlife will be. Only a handful of mortal heroes in Greek and Roman mythology were ever able to set foot in the Underworld and make it back to the land of the living. These include Hercules, Aeneas and Orpheus.

When you first get to the Underworld, you have to cross the black river Acheron on a ferry that is rowed by the mysterious, cloaked oarsman Charon. Both Greek and Roman families would place a coin in the mouth of their dead relatives before they were cremated, so that they had the money needed for Charon's fare. On the other side of the river Acheron, you come face-to-face with one of the most fearsome beasts in mythology: the ferocious, three-headed guard dog Cerberus. In the dark region of Erebus that lies beyond is the river Lethe, from which dead souls drink to forget their earthly lives. Finally, in front of the Palace of Hades, your life is judged and your place in the afterlife is determined. For the lucky ones, it is an eternity in the pleasure and the beauty of Elysium, and for others it's down to Tartarus, the darkest and cruellest place in the Underworld. The Elysian fields now give their name to the most famous street in Paris, the Champs-Élysées.

One unfortunate man assigned to Tartarus for the rest of time is Sisyphus. He tried to avoid his own death by capturing the death messenger that came for him. Hades looks very unkindly on those who attempt to cheat death, and so sets Sisyphus an eternity of torture, in which he must continually push a huge boulder up to the top of a vast mountain. Each time he is moments from the top, the boulder falls back to the bottom and Sisyphus must start again. It is for him that we refer to a Sisyphean task, one which feels impossible to complete.

Another miserable man who was judged unfavourably by Hades is the king Tantalus. Originally loved by the gods, Tantalus had the unusual privilege for a mortal to be able to dine with them on Mount Olympus. Despite this honour, Tantalus doubts the gods and their wisdom. In an extraordinary test of their powers, he kills his own son, Pelops, and cooks him into one of the dishes served at a divine dinner party. The gods see his deception immediately – only Demeter eats part of the boy in her distracted grief at losing her daughter Persephone. Pelops is brought back to life, but Tantalus is condemned to an eternity in Tartarus. He must stand forever in a pool of clear, refreshing water, surrounded by trees heavy with ripe fruit. But each time he bends down to drink from the pool, the water recedes just out of reach; and each time he lifts his hand to grab one of the fruits above him, the branches rise beyond his grasp. His eternal, unsatisfied hunger and thirst give us the English word 'tantalizing'.

Hestia – Vesta

Hestia is the sister of Zeus, Hades and Poseidon, and she is the goddess of the hearth – which is what her name means in Greek. The Roman name for this goddess, Vesta, is an evolution of the same word. For Greek and Roman society, the hearth really was the heart of the home. It represented warmth throughout the year, and was where food was prepared. It became synonymous with the home itself and the protection that it provided. In Greek tragedy, Agamemnon is murdered at the hearth of the Palace of Mycenae. As the very symbol of protection and of the seat of Mycenae itself, the location of the murder makes it even more gut-wrenching.

There are very few temples in Hestia's honour, but the hearth in every home was seen as a dedication to this one goddess. One very notable temple for her does exist in the Roman Forum. In this Temple of Vesta, as the Romans called it, a flame burned continuously to symbolize her protection over the Roman people. Extinguishing the flame would have meant the end of the Roman Empire, and so it was carefully guarded by the six Vestal Virgins. The role was a huge honour given to priestesses, who could retain the position for the next thirty years, if their own honour was never brought into question.

Otherwise, Hestia's very level-headed and protective character means she doesn't appear in many mythological stories; she doesn't have the traits of drama, jealousy and revenge that many of the others do. In fact, even in ancient times, she is often considered not to be one of the key twelve

Olympian gods. On one of the friezes from the Parthenon in Athens, the twelve Olympians include Dionysus instead of Hestia. Nonetheless, her importance in representing womanhood, modesty and protection gave her a special place in the daily lives of both Greek and Roman citizens.

Demeter – Ceres

Demeter is the goddess of agriculture, fertility and the harvest, and is often depicted with wheat or corn. In a civilization that depended on the success of crops from one season to the next, she played an important role in ancient religion. The Roman version of this goddess – Ceres – gives us the English word 'cereal'. Demeter's biggest impact in ancient mythology comes as a result of the abduction of her daughter Persephone by Hades.

Persephone is out in a meadow with her friend, the nymph Sion. The young daughter of Demeter and Zeus spots an utterly bewitching narcissus flower in the distance and wanders away from her friend to take a closer look. As she bends down to pick it up, the ground opens up to reveal the dark god of the Underworld himself; Hades reaches out and grabs the powerless girl.

A horrendous scream sounds up to the heavens. The olive trees shake and the mountains tremble with Persephone's call for help to Zeus. But no one hears her cries other than Sion, who saw Persephone's sudden disappearance. Hades throws Persephone into his golden chariot, and cracks the whip for his shadowy horses to speed away. Sion can do nothing but fall to the ground and weep. In fact, she cries so much that she creates the river Sion.

Zeus is deaf to the screams calling his name – perhaps because he placed that enticing flower for his daughter to find in the first place. His brother Hades loves the girl, but knows no mother would approve of their daughter marrying the king of the dead, so Zeus gets involved, ensuring that the narcissus lures Persephone to a spot where Hades can abduct her.

Demeter is beside herself with grief as she searches for her daughter. The mortals on Earth know that they need to keep Demeter in good spirits, as she provides food and vegetation. They build a vast temple in her honour for prayers and sacrifices to bring bountiful harvests. But Demeter is inconsolable, wasting away as she laments her darling daughter.

In her grief, the Earth suffers: not a single seed sprouts, despite humankind's efforts. The famine gets so bad that Zeus sends god after god to coax Demeter from isolation, but nothing works – all she wants is Persephone. Finally, Zeus sends the messenger god Hermes to convince Hades to release his bride and save the mortals from famine. Hades surprisingly agrees, telling Persephone: 'Go to your mother – she needs you now.' Without her realizing, Hades gives her six pomegranate seeds, a powerful signal that he now owns her in the Underworld. Once she eats from his food, she belongs to the land of the dead.

Persephone joyfully returns to her mother, and Demeter's

mood lifts. Instantly, vegetation flourishes and fertility spreads across the world. Mother and daughter reconcile with the other gods, but Zeus must reach a compromise, aware that Hades has lost his bride. Zeus asks his daughter where she would like to live, and it is clear that the fruit from Hades' hand has sealed their bond.

'Hades has been really kind to me,' Persephone tells her father. 'I really want to be by my husband's side.'

After such abject grief, Demeter can barely contain her rage. Darkness surrounds her, and Zeus realizes he must act before the world starves again. He decrees that Persephone will spend half the year in the Underworld with Hades, and the other half with Demeter on Mount Olympus. Seeing her daughter's happiness, Demeter agrees, though her grief remains. So for half the year, she stops crops from growing no matter how much effort humankind puts into the fields. But when reunited with Persephone, there is abundant growth across the world. Demeter teaches humanity the proper rituals and prayers to honour the life-giving riches she bestows on the Earth, and only those who conduct these rites will be able to feed in the Underworld after they have died.

Poseidon – Neptune

Poseidon is the very powerful brother of Zeus, matching his defiant decision-making and influence on humankind. He is the god of the seas, making him a hugely important deity for the seafarers that helped make the Greek and Roman civilizations so mighty. Often depicted with his trident and the white horses of the ocean, one blow from his weapon could raise a storm or cause an earthquake.

However, it isn't just in the sea that Poseidon has influence. He appears in both the *Iliad* and the *Odyssey* by Greek poet Homer, playing a significant role in the ten-year Trojan War. The combined armies from across Greece are besieging the city of Troy in an attempt to win back Queen Helen, who has been stolen from the Greeks. Zeus has ordered the gods to stop meddling in the tragic war that has cost so many lives, but they can't help themselves. When the Greeks are suffering losses at the hands of the Trojans, Poseidon rides his golden chariot, pulled by his powerful white horses. He parts the seas and drives at speed to the Greek army. There he disguises himself as one of their men, gives them encouragement and even fights with them.

Poseidon is the father of the mighty, one-eyed Cyclops that Odysseus eventually defeats. As Odysseus is sailing away from the Cyclops' cave with the few men that were not killed, he shouts back to the monster that he is Odysseus, king of Ithaca. Without missing a beat, the mountain-sized Cyclops prays to his father, Poseidon, to make Odysseus' journey home from the Trojan War even harder than it already has been. It is Poseidon who blows Odysseus even further off course, and who ensures that Odysseus loses every last man on his way.

Ares – Mars

Ares is the violent god of war. He is the son of Zeus and Hera, but has a problematic reputation among the gods and even in Greek society. Other gods are associated with war, but in very different ways. Athena represents wisdom, strategy and protection in battle, and Hephaestus masters the art of creating unrivalled armour and weaponry. Contrary to this, Ares has the bloodlust of vicious battle, and is often accompanied by his sons Deimos ('Terror') and Phobos ('Fear'). The Romans, however, had a more favourable view of this god, whom they named Mars. Perhaps it is because the skill and precision of the Roman army created a sense of honour and pride in the ever-growing empire that the army was effectively building. The Roman name Mars gives us the English word 'martial' (as in *martial arts*). The forenames Mark and Martin, as well as the month of March, are named in this god's honour.

He is equally troublesome off the battlefield as he is on it, seeding discord and conflict wherever he goes, and even having a not-so-secret affair with the love goddess Aphrodite, despite her being married to his brother Hephaestus. It is the sun god Helios who spies Ares and Aphrodite making love on Hephaestus' bed, and who goes to tell him of the affair. As the master smith of the gods, Hephaestus fashions a trap to catch the lovers. He makes a net so fine that it is invisible and imperceptible to the touch. Hephaestus lays the net on his own bed and waits. When Ares and Aphrodite lie on the bed again, they get caught up in the fine net and are unable to move. Hephaestus invites the whole pantheon of gods to come and see the two lovers trapped in their humiliating tryst.

Ares helps to found the city of Thebes, known for its fierce warriors. Before the city state is founded, Ares creates a bloodthirsty dragon to terrorize the nearby population. The hero Cadmus is wandering the world in search of his sister, Europa, who has been abducted by Zeus, when he comes across a water spring that is being guarded by the serpentine dragon. Cadmus is able to kill the beast with a rock, not realizing he has incurred the wrath of the most violent of the gods. Wise and temperate Athena advises Cadmus to bury the dragon's teeth, from which emerge an army of fierce warriors known as the Spartoi. They all immediately start fighting and killing one another, leaving just five men that help Cadmus found the city of Thebes.

Ares is so angered by the death of his scaly dragon that he forces Cadmus to work as his slave for eight years. At the end of that punishment, he rewards him with the hand in marriage of his daughter Harmonia. The two live a long life, but Cadmus is eventually turned into a snake by the vengeful Ares. Seeing her husband grow scales and transform into a hideous snake, Harmonia successfully pleads to be given the same tragic fate.

Hephaestus – Vulcan

Hephaestus is the master craftsman of the gods. The son of Zeus and Hera is the god of fire, smiths and masonry. He is the go-to artisan for the greatest armour, weapons and metalwork in classical mythology. He crafts Achilles' shield, Hercules' armour, Artemis' hunting arrows, Apollo's chariot, Zeus' protective aegis shield and Athena's spear, to name a few. His Roman name, Vulcan, gives us the English word 'volcano', whose fiery depths were said to represent the god's glowing hot forge. He is often depicted with the hammer, tongs or other tools of his smithing craft, and is lame with a deformed foot. As such, he is sometimes shown riding a donkey.

The myths around him contradict one another, but one common theme remains: he is thrown off Mount Olympus and lives a life separate from the other Olympians, even though they respect his artistry and skill. In one story, his mother, Hera, is disgusted when she discovers his deformed foot after his birth. He is not deemed fit for the Olympians and she casts him off the mountain. He lands in the sea, and is luckily saved and raised by Eurynome and Thetis (mother of Achilles) on the volcanic island of Lemnos – where he hones his skill as master craftsman.

In another version of the myth, Hephaestus is flung down from Mount Olympus as a fully grown god, resulting in his leg injury. Zeus is angered at his wife Hera for setting a storm on Hercules as he returns from Troy. Zeus hangs Hera in chains from Mount Olympus as a punishment.

When Hephaestus rushes to his mother's rescue, Zeus grabs him by the leg and hurls him down. He falls for one full day from the mountain down to Earth, finally landing on the island of Lemnos.

He is married to the goddess of love and lust, Aphrodite. The contrast of her allure, beauty and sex appeal with his deformity and hard labour would have been a comic punchline to Greek and Roman audiences.

Athena – Minerva

Athena is the goddess of wisdom and war. Her role is often as a guide to the mythological heroes of ancient legends, appearing to Aeneas, Hercules or Odysseus in their hour of need. She whispers wise advice, emboldens them in battle, or talks them out of rash acts of violence and revenge. She is often depicted with an owl, the animal that even today we consider to symbolize wisdom because of its association with Athena. Much sculpture and art shows her ready for war, wearing a helmet, breastplate or carrying Zeus' protective aegis shield. Her armour can be engraved with the snaky head of Medusa, whom Athena first turned into a monster, and whom she helped Perseus to behead.

Athena is the daughter of Zeus, from his earlier marriage to Metis. In typical fashion, Zeus had heard a prophecy that his offspring would grow up to usurp his power, so he swallowed Metis and her unborn child in one go. However, the powerful Athena sprang forth from Zeus' head, fully grown and carrying a spear ready for war. It shouldn't be surprising that Athena was most keenly worshipped in the city of Athens, which is named after the goddess. On top of the Acropolis, the prominent hill in the centre of the city, is perhaps the most famous temple of the Ancient Greek world: the Parthenon. Its name means 'the Maiden', as it was dedicated to the virgin goddess Athena. In 438 BC, a colossal statue of Athena was installed inside the Parthenon, standing 12 metres (about 40 feet) tall. The glistening gold and ivory statue showed her holding a spear in one hand, a small statue of the victory goddess Nike in the other hand, wearing her trademark helmet, and standing beside the aegis shield and a large snake.

Both Athena and Poseidon vied to have the city of Athens dedicated to them. Poseidon struck the ground with his heavy trident, and seawater poured forth from a spring in the city. Athena's offering to the city was in planting its very first olive tree, and she was deemed the worthy winner.

Hermes – Mercury

Hermes is the messenger god, born from Zeus' union with Maia, one of Atlas' daughters. He is depicted as a young man in a cap, wearing winged sandals, and he carries a caduceus – a staff with two snakes entwined around it. He delivers messages between the gods, passing on news for celebration as well as thunderous decrees from Zeus.

A bronze statue of Hermes by Giovanni Bologna.

He also guides the dead down into the Underworld to the banks of the Acheron river.

Even as a baby, Hermes' mischievous character is evident. The day after he is born, he escapes his mother Maia's arms and wanders into the night. He eats the meat from the inside of a turtle shell, to which he attaches reeds and animal sinews, creating the first ever lyre. He wanders on and comes across herds of cattle that belong to his half-brother Apollo, which he decides to steal. Apollo chases down the young god, not fooled by his innocent appearance, and hauls him in front of mighty Zeus to settle the matter. Zeus orders Hermes to return the cattle, but he instead offers Apollo the tortoise-shell lyre. It is from this gift that Apollo becomes the superbly skilled musician and god of music.

Artemis – Diana

Artemis is the goddess of hunting and wildlife, and is usually depicted with her bow and arrows, or with wild animals. She is the twin sister of Apollo, born of Zeus and Leto. Zeus' wife Hera is so enraged by yet another pregnant mistress that she disallows Leto from giving birth on any land. Leto travels across Greece and is turned away again and again. Finally, she finds the floating island of Delos, where the twins are born.

During the fifth century BC, Delos was a powerful island in the trade of goods and people across the Mediterranean and beyond, with up to ten thousand slaves being sold there on a single day. A decree was issued prohibiting anyone from being born or dying on Delos, in order to preserve its sacred status in Greek religion. Even for modern-day Greeks, Delos holds spiritual significance, and the birth and death ban remains a widely held belief to this day.

The small island of Delos, a UNESCO World Heritage Site, boasts phenomenal ruins of an ancient city that you can wander through. From the late 1960s onwards, hippies from nearby Mykonos would arrive on fishing boats during full moons to dance on this magical island. Its status as a spiritual place from the birth of Artemis and Apollo lives on.

Artemis is highly protective of her chastity, and it costs at least one man his life. A prince of Thebes, Actaeon, is hunting when he comes across the goddess of the hunt herself, bathing in a river. She is so outraged that he has seen her divine nudity that she turns him into a deer. Immediately, his dogs don't recognize their own master, and they turn on him, tearing him limb from limb.

Her chastity is challenged again when she meets the great hunter Orion. One version of the myth describes how she starts to fall for the attractive man. Her brother Apollo spots the potential danger, and steps in to save Artemis' honour. Orion goes swimming in a vast lake one day, and swims out so far that his head is just a dot on the horizon. Apollo challenges his sister to an archery contest, betting that she couldn't hit that little speck in the distance. Drawn into the game, she ends up killing Orion with one perfectly delivered arrow. In her grief, she asks Zeus to set Orion into the night sky as the constellation that still bears his name today.

Apollo

Apollo is the god of art, culture, music and prophecy. He is the twin brother of hunter goddess Artemis, and he shares her skill in archery. You can recognize him as an attractive god, often with a wreath of laurel around his head, a lyre or his bow and arrows. He is one of the only gods to have the same name in both Greek and Roman traditions.

An unusual depiction of Apollo as a red figure painted on a white
background in this shallow bowl (cylix), 480–460 BC, Delphi.

The most famous temple to Apollo is the one at Delphi,
where a priestess known as the Oracle of Delphi would
enter a trance and speak in tongues, delivering profound
prophecies to eager visitors from the seventh century BC
onwards. On a column inside the temple was inscribed
the famous Delphic maxim 'Know Thyself', an invitation
to the self-awareness that is needed if you want to get the
most from a visit to the oracle.

Before the Oracle of Delphi was dedicated to Apollo, it
was guarded by a huge serpentine dragon called Python,
placed there by the Earth mother Gaia. Apollo wants to
help the people of Delphi, and he kills the ferocious beast

by raining his arrows down upon it. Python gasps its last breaths, writhing around in agony as it dies. The Greeks called the priestess at the Temple of Apollo the Pythia, in commemoration of Apollo's defeat of Python. It is from this monster that python snakes are named.

Apollo had been instrumental in building the city of Troy, and so he fiercely defends it during the ten-year Trojan War, even though many of the other Olympians are assisting the Greeks on the other side in that war. During that time, Apollo falls in love with a Trojan princess called Cassandra, and endows her with the gift of prophecy. When she continues to refuse his advances, he curses her so that no one will ever believe her predictions. She constantly warns the people of her city that Troy will fall, and she tells them not to trust the Trojan Horse – a gift from the Greeks – but her words fall on deaf ears.

Another unrequited love of Apollo is that of young nymph Daphne. He pursues her relentlessly, despite her protestations against him. He chases her until she can feel his breath in her hair. As Apollo reaches out to grab the poor girl, she casts a prayer out to her father, a river god, and pleads for her beauty to be undone. In that moment, her body hardens, tree bark grows over her chest, her flowing hair turns to leaves, and her waving limbs become branches in the wind. Her running feet stick fast into the ground with thick roots, and she has become the laurel tree, which is the meaning of the name Daphne. Apollo still admires her beauty in tree form, and decrees that laurel leaves must be worn around the head of all the winning athletes in the

Pythian Games that are held in his honour at Delphi. It is a tradition that was replicated for the medal winners at the 2004 Olympic Games in Athens.

Dionysus – Bacchus

Dionysus is the god of wine, wine-making and general festivities. In Roman religion, he was called Bacchus, and the term 'bacchanalian' is used in English today to describe a boozy party. He is one of the most commonly depicted gods in ancient art, since he is the embodiment of celebration and joy, although the negative sides of Dionysus' wine were part of the myths even in ancient times. He is instantly recognizable by the grape vines and wine cups that surround his sculptures and paintings, and is sometimes seen riding leopards and large cats.

As one of the earliest gods to appear in Greek myth, there are several competing versions of the stories that surround him. He is the result of another one of Zeus' more than one hundred affairs, this time with Semele. She is the daughter of Cadmus, who founded the city of Thebes after searching for his sister Europa, and she becomes pregnant by Zeus.

Hera acts as the vengeful, scorned wife once more, and disguises herself as Semele's nurse. She convinces Semele to ask her lover to prove that he is indeed Zeus by appearing to her in his true, divine form. Hera knows that no mortal will be able to survive such a vision. Semele first asks Zeus to promise that he will grant one wish that she makes of him, which he agrees. Then comes the request: that he reveals himself to her in his true appearance. Having made the promise and being unable to decline, Zeus takes on his divine form. From his simple human shape, he suddenly lifts up into the heavens, becomes the very clouds and the rain, and he turns into the thunder and lightning that he commands. This is how he now stands before her.

Semele is unable to cope with such a blazing vision and she dies at the exposure to the god of the skies. Zeus is able to save the unborn Dionysus and sew him into his own thigh, from where he is born again after some time. In this way, Dionysus is said to have been born twice: once from Semele and again from Zeus' thigh.

Aphrodite – Venus

Aphrodite is the goddess of love and sexual desire. She embodies the passion, lust and destruction that can come with all the facets of an emotion as complicated and intense as love. She is married to Hephaestus, the god of fire, and is having an affair with the warmongering Ares. She is either the daughter of Uranus, born when his testicles are hurled into the frothing sea by Cronus, or she is the daughter of Zeus and the goddess Dione. Either way, she becomes one of the key twelve Olympian gods in ancient mythology and features widely in the legends that surround them. Ancient statues and art of the goddess show her incredible beauty, and usually in various stages of undress.

In one story, Aphrodite punishes a young girl, Myrrha, by making her fall in love with her own father, King Cinyras. The girl creeps into his room at night, and sleeps with him before he can discover her identity. When the truth comes out, the king is so disgusted that he sets out to kill his daughter. She flees and begs with the gods for a disguise so that her father doesn't find her. She is transformed into the first myrrh tree, but is nonetheless pregnant and gives birth to a son, the young Adonis.

Aphrodite gives the baby to Persephone to look after. He grows into a very handsome young man, and soon the two goddesses are fighting over which of them should be his lover. Zeus decrees that Adonis should spend a third of the year with Aphrodite, a third of the year with Persephone, and decide for himself with which goddess he will spend the remaining third of the year. When the time comes, he spends more time with Aphrodite, incurring the jealousy of her other lover, the war god Ares. Disguised as a boar, Ares charges the handsome Adonis and gores him in the thigh with a sharp tusk.

Aphrodite finds Adonis bleeding to death, and she holds him in her arms. Red blood is dripping down his snow-white skin, and his eyes start to glaze over. As the redness leaves his lips, Aphrodite places her own lips there one final time. The kiss dies upon his skin and is gone; he never knows that he was kissed.

CHAPTER 2

HEROES, HEROINES AND MONSTERS

Pandora

In Greek mythology, Pandora is the first mortal woman that existed. Her creation is specifically designed to challenge the men that had already been brought into existence. The fire god Prometheus had gone behind Zeus' back and had brought fire from the heavens and given it to mankind. Zeus feared humanity becoming too powerful, so in retaliation he commissioned Hephaestus, blacksmith to the gods, to fashion a woman out of clay.

All the gods come together to help create the ultimate obstacle to man's progress. Aphrodite, goddess of love, gives her beauty and desire; Athena gives her clothing and skills in weaving; Hermes, the messenger god, gives her the power of deceitful language; others give her jewellery and adorn her with garlands. The name *Pandora* means 'all gifted', perhaps for all the gifts that she has been given, or perhaps for the gifts she inadvertently gives to mankind.

Zeus delivers Pandora to Prometheus' foolish brother Epimetheus. The young man marries her, despite the warnings of Prometheus, and she is gifted a jar from Zeus that contains all the evils and misery of the world. Pandora opens the jar, releasing the swarm of evil spirits into the

It is only a sixteenth-century mistranslation that changed Pandora's jar into Pandora's box, which is the name that has endured in the retelling of her story.

world, which will plague mankind for eternity. Only one spirit is unable to escape: Elpis (Hope) is the single blessing left to mankind upon Zeus' wish. Despite all the difficulties and miseries we face, we will always have Hope to guide us.

Hercules

Hercules is the archetypal mythological hero: brave, muscly and immortal. He is one of the 115 or so illegitimate children of Zeus, and so incurs the lifelong wrath of Zeus' wife Hera. Even naming the child Heracles in Greek, meaning 'the glory of Hera', doesn't mollify her resentment of him. When he is a baby, Hera sends two snakes into Hercules' cot, which he

The emperor Commodus commissioned this statue of himself styled as Hercules, complete with lion head skin and club, c. AD 192.

immediately dispatches. His mother finds him playing with them like two limp dolls. This clearly is no ordinary child.

When he grows into adulthood, Hera drives Hercules into a mad frenzy, in which he kills his wife and children. Horrified and sickened by his own actions, he seeks forgiveness and advice from the wise Oracle of Delphi. It is decreed that Hercules must enter a decade of servitude under King Eurystheus of Tiryns, and must undertake any task that the king orders. Only then will he be offered the immortality that his demigod status deserves. Once again, Hera intervenes, and she convinces King Eurystheus to order impossible tasks for the hero to complete. These are known as the Twelve Labours of Hercules, from where we still refer to a Herculean task today for anything that feels difficult or impossible to achieve.

THE TWELVE LABOURS

Kill the Nemean Lion

This gigantic lion has claws of solid bronze and skin that Hercules' arrows cannot pierce. Hercules beats it with his huge club and corners it in a cave. Here, he can strangle it until it struggles no more. Hercules is often depicted holding a club and wearing the lion's skin.

Kill the Lernaean Hydra

This horrendous monster guards an entrance to the Underworld. Each time Hercules cuts off one of its many snake heads, a new one grows in its place. The hero uses a burning torch to cauterize each wound, preventing the regrowth of heads. Once the monster is killed, he dips his arrows into its poisonous blood to help with his later labours.

Capture the Ceryneian Hind

This golden-horned deer is sacred to the goddess Artemis. Hercules chases it for an entire year before he's able to get his hands on it, breaking off one antler in the struggle. Artemis allows him to borrow the sacred animal just long enough to present to King Eurystheus and to complete his task.

Capture the Erymanthian Boar

This violent beast has killed many people. Hercules chases the animal up the sides of Mount Erymanthos, driving it eventually into deep snow. There, he is able to capture it in a net.

Clean the Augean Stables

The herd of 3,000 cattle belongs to King Augeas. Hercules must muck out their stables – a duty that has been neglected for thirty years. The hero diverts two rivers to flow directly through the stables and wash away the dung in one go.

Kill the Stymphalian Birds

These man-eating birds around Lake Stymphalis have solid bronze beaks and feathers that they can shoot like arrows. Hercules shakes a noisy rattle gifted to him by Athena and Hephaestus, startling the birds into the air, where they are an easy target for him.

Capture the Cretan Bull

This huge white bull is the father of the gruesome Minotaur (see page 65). Hercules wrestles the beast with his bare hands and offers it as a sacrifice to Hera. Not wanting to acknowledge Hercules' mounting victories, she rebuffs the offer and the bull is released.

Take the Mares of Diomedes

These man-eating horses of King Diomedes have a thirst for blood. Hercules leaves his friend Abderus to guard them while the hero fights off – and ultimately kills – Diomedes. Returning to the horses, Hercules sees they have eaten Abderus and are still in a frenzy for flesh. He feeds the king's body to the savage beasts, calming them enough to be muzzled and led away by the hero.

Steal the Girdle of Hippolyta

Hippolyta is the queen of the Amazons, a race of warrior women that live by the Black Sea. Her belt is a symbol of her power among the warriors, and she is at first quite willing to give it to Hercules. Hera steps in and spreads a rumour that the hero is after the queen as well as her belt. The Amazons attack and Hippolyta is killed by Hercules, allowing him to easily take the girdle.

Bring the Cattle of Geryon

Geryon is a three-headed, three-bodied monster, and owner of a herd of cows coloured red by the setting sun of the west. Hercules uses an arrow dipped in the blood of the Hydra to kill monstrous Geryon, then leads the herd away.

Obtain the Apples of the Hesperides

These golden apples are sacred to Hera and grant immortality to anyone who should eat them. The apple tree is guarded by three nymphs, the Hesperides. Hercules goes via their father, Atlas, in the hope that he can convince his daughters to give up some of their precious fruit. Atlas has been sentenced by the gods to hold up the heavens for eternity, so Hercules offers to take up the weight of the heavens temporarily. Atlas fetches three of the golden apples from his daughters, but on his return, is tricked by Hercules into taking up the burden once more.

Capture Cerberus

The three-headed dog that guards the Underworld is not to be messed with. Hercules must enter the world of the dead, where he throws his arms around the beast's three necks long enough to subdue him and lead him back up to King Eurystheus. Hercules is absolved of his terrible crimes and gifted immortality.

The Trojan Horse

Perhaps one of the most well-known legends of the classical world, the story of the Trojan Horse is told in both Greek and Roman literature. The Trojan War has been raging for nearly a decade. The Greek army is camped out on the plains outside the high walls of the city of Troy, and they are nearly broken by the years of battle. With the help of the goddess Athena, they construct a huge wooden horse and conceal forty of their strongest soldiers in its hollow belly. The rest of the Greek army retreats to an offshore island, leaving behind their weapons, tents and equipment.

The Trojan people don't know what to make of this hasty retreat after so many years of war. They fight among themselves about what to do with the wooden horse that stands before their city gates. One priest of Poseidon, Laocoön, argues strongly against touching this gift from the enemy army: 'I fear Greeks, even those bearing gifts!' he cries.

He hurls a spear into the side of the horse, killing one Greek inside. No one hears the death cry from within, because at the same moment there is a commotion in the crowd. A captured Greek boy is being pushed through the mob. He explains how the Greeks all fled and left this offering to Athena, and how disregarding it will lead to the destruction of Troy. Two snaking serpents come slinking through the frothing sea. The crowd scatters as the monsters descend on Laocoön's two small sons. The priest tries in vain to save his boys, but all three of them are crushed by the beasts. The Trojans need no more convincing to heave the mighty wooden horse within the city walls, and they hold a huge celebration to honour Athena and the end of the war.

That night, while the Trojans sleep off their celebrations, they don't hear the Greek soldiers creeping out of the belly of the horse, and they don't hear the Greek army returning ashore. Nor do they hear their city gates being opened from within, and thousands of enemy soldiers pouring into their streets. The city of Troy is razed to the ground, their king Priam is murdered, and their homes are torched. The Greeks are finally victorious after ten long years of war, and the few Trojans that remain flee or are captured.

Medusa

The snake-haired Medusa is a well-known image of the classical world. Early depictions don't include the famous serpentine hair, instead showing her with large wings, a hideous face and tusks. One look at her frightful face will turn any person into stone. It is said that she used to be the very embodiment of beauty, known particularly for her gorgeous hair, resulting in the god of the seas, Poseidon, violating her in a temple of Athena. That goddess was so affronted by the deed that she punished Medusa for her beauty – rather than Poseidon for his violation – and turned her into the hideous Gorgon we've come to know.

King Acrisius of Argos is given a terrible omen that a grandson will grow up to kill him. He's so terrified of the prophecy that he locks his daughter Danaë in an underground bronze chamber to prevent her from ever bearing a son. But the king of the gods, Zeus, disguises himself as a golden rain that showers down onto her and gives her a son, Perseus. Horrified that the omen may yet come true, King Acrisius casts both his daughter and his grandson into the sea inside a locked chest.

Against all odds, the pair wash ashore on the island of

Seriphos, where Perseus grows up into a young man. On the island, a man called Polydectes falls in love with Danaë and decides that it is time to get rid of her son Perseus. Polydectes sets the hero a seemingly impossible task: bring back the head of the hideous Medusa.

Perseus prays to the gods Athena and Hermes for guidance on how to kill the ferocious monster. They tell him to travel to the very ends of the known world to the Hesperides nymphs. The nymphs furnish him with the weapons he will need: winged sandals from the messenger god Hermes, a mighty diamond sword from Zeus, a pouch in which to carry the decapitated head of Medusa – to avoid one glance turning him to stone even in death – and the invisibility helmet from Hades of the Underworld.

Perseus finds Medusa asleep in a cave, surrounded by other Gorgons. Guided by the gods, he dare not look directly at the monster, but glances instead at the reflection of her in the shimmering bronze shield strapped to one arm. Around her head are entwined black dragon scales and sinuous serpentine hair, and huge tusks jut out from her hideous mouth. She rests on solid bronze hands and her mighty, golden wings are folded behind her.

Athena is looking down on the hero. She strengthens his hand and guides him towards Medusa while he looks only at the reflected image. He raises the magnificent diamond sword and with all his strength cuts off her deadly head. The Gorgons around her awake with screeches that reverberate about the cave and shake the ground. In a moment, Perseus grabs the blood-soaked head and stashes it in his pouch. He puts on the invisibility helmet once more to make his escape.

Perseus eventually makes his way home, not just to the island of Seriphos, but to his rightful home of Argos. King Acrisius, who cast Perseus out to sea all those years ago, is terrified that the oracle's prophecy will come to pass – that he will be killed by his own grandson – and the king flees to the other side of Greece. But you cannot run from your fate, and Perseus eventually kills the king.

For her guidance in his seemingly impossible task, Perseus offers the head of Medusa to the goddess Athena, who immortalizes the serpentine monster in her shield. Many of the depictions of Athena in art and sculpture show her bearing the shape of Medusa's head in her armour.

The Minotaur

Greece as we know it today didn't exist as one entity, and instead was a collection of many different city states, each with its own king, but nonetheless unified through similar languages centred on Athens. Down in Crete, King Minos was a fearful ruler, and following a disagreement with Athens, he demanded that seven young men and seven young women each year boarded a black-sailed ship to Crete, where they were sacrificed to the Minotaur. This beast was half-man and half-bull, as a result of a union between a bull and either Europa or Pasiphaë, depending on which myth you believe. The monster lived hidden away in King Minos' inescapable labyrinth.

The Greek hero Theseus wants to put an end to the annual horror and to be a hero among his people, and so volunteers himself as one of the seven young men. When in Minos' palace in Knossos (the ruins of which you can still visit today), Theseus is visited by Minos' daughter Ariadne. She gives him a ball of silk thread and tells him to unwind it as he travels through the labyrinth to help him easily find his way out. He bravely kills the Minotaur and takes Ariadne home with him – although he is then told by the god Dionysus to leave her on the island of Naxos, since the god wants her for his own bride.

In his grief at losing Ariadne, Theseus returns to Athens and forgets to change the sails of the ship from black to white. Doing so would indicate that he had triumphed over the Minotaur. King Aegeus sees the ship approaching from a distance and fears the worst when he spies the black sails: that Theseus has been killed and that the Minotaur's terrible rampage continues. Without waiting to confirm his concerns, Aegeus hurls himself into the sea that even now bears his name.

Theseus becomes king of Athens, and unifies all the Attic states into one notional country. Since this unification actually took place over a number of centuries, we can assume the myth of Theseus to be an allegory of the 'Greekness' he embodied. Crete's king Minos was known for his barbaric and draconian punishments, so it is easy to see how a foreign king in a huge sprawling palace could be muddled into a mythical beast living in a confusing labyrinth, of which there is no evidence in Knossos. In slaying the barbaric non-Greek monster and overcoming the Cretan king, the hero Theseus acts as a perfectly virile personification of the Greek people.

Cerberus

Much of classical mythology deals with the subject of death. When people have been unable to explain the heartache of grief, nor to understand what happens to our loved ones after they die, civilizations the world over have created rich mythologies to make sense of the inexplicable. It is far easier to believe a story of the Underworld, inhabited by gods, monsters and spirits, than it is to fathom the sudden sorrow of death.

Originating in Greek mythology, Cerberus is a ferocious, three-headed dog that guards one gate in the Underworld. Some ancient literature describes him as having fifty or a hundred heads, a serpent's tail, or snakes coming out of his back. But it is the three-headed image that has endured and inspired artists and authors all the way up to J. K. Rowling.

Cerberus is the brother of some other well-known, multi-headed beasts in Greek mythology: the nine-headed Lernaean Hydra, the two-headed guard dog of the Cattle of Geryon, and the lion-goat-snake hybrid Chimera. This places him in quite some clan of ferocious foes. Both Cerberus and the Hydra are targets of Hercules in his famous Twelve Labours.

What makes Cerberus all the more dreadful to imagine is that his gate is well within the land of the dead. It is not some entrance to the Underworld that he guards – many landmarks, caves and lakes across the Greek and Roman worlds were thought to be such entrances – but it is a gate on the other side of the river Acheron in the land of Hades. So, if you ever set eyes on the beast, you're already likely to be well beyond saving.

The Cyclops

Odysseus is a Greek king and military leader. After the Greeks conquer the city of Troy following the ten-year war, their troubles are far from over. Odysseus must guide his fleet of twelve ships for a further ten years as they attempt to make their way home to the island of Ithaca. Constantly blown off course and held captive in strange lands, they encounter beasts, gods and monsters along the way.

On one unfamiliar shore, they hear the voices of towering, one-eyed Cyclops giants. The land is uncultivated, there are no harbours for ships, and there are no signs of a civilized society. Even in this lawless place, there is one Cyclops who is an outcast from the rest: the belligerent Polyphemus, as much a colossal mountain as he is a man. This giant lives alone in a huge, rocky cave, away from the others.

Odysseus takes twelve of his strongest warriors to visit the Cyclops, in the hope that they will be offered a guest's welcome and helped on their hard-fought journey home.

Inside the gigantic cave, they are not greeted with the warmth they were hoping for: Polyphemus grabs two of Odysseus' men, hammers their heads on the ground and picks their limbs apart before sucking the bodies clean like a chicken wing. Each day, the beastly giant leads his flock of vast sheep out of the cave to pasture, and heaves a huge boulder across the entrance to the cave. When he returns with the sheep at the end of each day, he devours more of Odysseus' men.

Odysseus hatches a plan. One evening, he steels himself to offer the giant some of the wine they have brought with them from their travels. He introduces himself to the Cyclops as 'Nobody'. Polyphemus gladly necks the undiluted drink and eventually collapses by his campfire. The remaining men take one of the Cyclops' staffs – a huge olive trunk – and harden one sharp end in the fire embers before driving it into the sleeping giant's one eye. It sizzles and hisses as he is blinded. The other Cyclops hear the cries from within the cave, only to be told by Polyphemus: 'Nobody has blinded me!'

The following morning, Odysseus and his men tie themselves to the undersides of the gigantic sheep, and are able to escape unnoticed as the blinded Cyclops feels his way around the cave. Once safe on their ships again, Odysseus cannot help but boast of his trickery. He calls out to the Cyclops that it was King Odysseus of Ithaca who blinded him and escaped his cave. It is a boast that will be costly: Polyphemus calls out to Poseidon, god of the seas, to make Odysseus' journey home even harder than it has been. The curse indeed comes true, and Odysseus loses every last man on his way, and he finds his homeland of Ithaca in ruin when he finally returns.

Paris

Paris was the prince of Troy and one of the most eligible bachelors of the classical world. Upon his birth, a prophecy foretold that he would grow up to bring about the destruction of his famous city, but neither his parents – King Priam and Queen Hecuba – nor their chief herdsman Agelaus could bring themselves to kill the baby. He was left on the cold sides of Mount Ida to die, but was looked after by a benevolent bear and survived. He was raised by Agelaus as a shepherd before his true identity was revealed and he returned to his place in the palace of Troy.

Paris holds a hugely important place in Greek mythology, as his actions bring about the terrible ten-year Trojan War. At the wedding of the goddess Thetis to the mortal Peleus, all the gods had been invited except for one: Eris, the goddess of discord. When she is turned away at the gates, Eris decides that she will make her presence known nonetheless. She casts a golden apple into the heavenly crowd, with just one word inscribed into it: καλλίστῃ (*kallistei*), 'for the prettiest one'.

It rolls to the feet of three goddesses: Hera, the wife of Zeus; Athena, goddess of wisdom; and Aphrodite, the goddess of love. Each of them feels they should lay claim to the golden apple, and so Zeus understandably avoids all involvement, sending them off to see Paris instead to make the unenviable decision. Each goddess promises the prince of Troy something in return for him favouring them in his decision. Hera offers him power over all of Europe and Asia; Athena offers him wisdom; and Aphrodite offers him the hand in marriage of the world's most beautiful woman, Helen of Sparta.

Paris gifts the apple to Aphrodite, and takes Helen with him to Troy. The only problem is that Helen is already married to Greek king Menelaus. It is this that instigates the fearful Trojan War, as the Greeks head over to retrieve their queen. The mythological war is the inspiration for so much of classical literature, art and sculpture, and acts as the backdrop to Homer's *Iliad* and *Odyssey*, many Greek tragic plays, and Virgil's *Aeneid*.

Achilles

Thetis and Peleus, whose marriage gave us the golden apple and led to the Trojan War, were the parents of Achilles. He is one of Greek mythology's leading heroes, and their victory in that war is largely credited to Achilles avenging the death of his lover Patroclus.

The goddess Thetis had caught the attention of both Zeus and his brother Poseidon, king of the seas. But when they heard the prophecy that she would bear a son who would become more powerful than his father, both the gods backed down. Instead, Zeus decided she should be married to the mortal man Peleus, so that the prophecy wouldn't be too threatening to their authority if it did come true. Thetis initially resists the marriage, taking on the form of a lion and a flame to avoid Peleus, but she is forced to relent.

When the demigod Achilles is born, he is mortal, unlike his mother, so the goddess fears for him. In her attempt to make him immortal, she takes him to the river Styx in the Underworld. It is this river that everyone must cross after their death, and Thetis holds her child by his ankle and dips him into its waters. It is said that every part of

A drinking cup, depicting Achilles bandaging the wound of his friend Patroclus, c. 500 BC.

him becomes immortal, except for the ankle that did not touch the water.

> Achilles' weakness gives us the expression 'Achilles heel'. Homer's *Iliad* doesn't mention his heel specifically, so it seems to be a later addition to the myths around the hero.

Thetis soon abandons her son and husband to return to the sea, from where she came, leaving Peleus to raise the boy. He sends Achilles to be educated by the centaur Chiron. The half-man, half-horse guide has previous experience training both Hercules and Jason, two of Ancient Greece's most heroic characters. He teaches Achilles the arts of hunting and music, and builds him into the extraordinary soldier and leader we come to know in Homer's works.

Romulus and Remus

One of the most famous myths from the Roman civilization is that of Romulus and Remus, the young boys who were raised by a wolf before founding the city of Rome. There are a few conflicting versions of the legend, but when you look at a nation's origin stories, you'll understand more about what they thought of themselves and how they wanted to be seen.

The legend goes that King Numitor ruled in Alba Longa, located south-east of modern-day Rome. His younger brother Amulius usurps the king, and to avoid any future heirs claiming their right to the throne, he forces Numitor's daughter Rhea Silvia into a life of chastity. However, Rhea becomes pregnant by Mars, the god of war, and gives birth to twins. Wanting to secure his power over Alba Longa, Amulius orders the young boys to be drowned in the river Tiber. However, Romulus and Remus float down the river and land at the site of the future city of Rome. They are initially suckled by a wolf and fed by a woodpecker, and ultimately are raised by a shepherd and his wife.

Eventually, the twins grow up, and gather an army of young shepherds to overthrow Amulius and reinstate their grandfather Numitor as the king of Alba Longa. They return to found their own city, but disagree about which of seven hills should be the site. Romulus builds walls around his proposed site, on the Palatine Hill, and Remus settles on the Aventine Hill. Romulus eventually kills his brother and the city is named in his honour, presumed to be in 753 BC.

The only thing left is to populate Rome with women, which Romulus does by stealing them against their will from nearby Sabinum – a scene depicted in countless works of Renaissance art as the rape of the Sabines. It certainly feels like strange beginnings for such a proud civilization. But perhaps it is this sense of pride to the point of arrogance that made the Romans so successful: their sense of superiority allowed them to take what they wanted and to expand the empire with great strength. Where

Alexander the Great failed with his Greek empire, the Romans were able to instil this glorious sense of belonging within its citizens that lasted a great deal longer. The violent myths of its origins perhaps gave the population a sense of entitlement that worked in the empire's favour.

The famous bronze sculpture of Romulus and Remus suckling their wolf foster mother, c. 500–480 BC.

CHAPTER 3

KINGS, QUEENS AND RULERS

GREEK RULERS

King Minos

Ancient Greece was not one nation in the way we might think of it now, but made up of many city states, each with its own king or queen, its own palace and city walls, its own customs, and with distinct regional dialects. Nonetheless, most of what we now call Greece spoke a version of the same language, shared mythology and a pantheon of gods, and there was a definite sense of Greekness with political and trading centres in Mycenae, on Delos, and finally in Athens from the fifth century BC. Many of the mythological characters from Ancient Greece were kings or queens of their own city state: King Odysseus of Ithaca, King Agamemnon of Mycenae and King Oedipus of Thebes. The Greek name for these states, the *polis*, gives us the English word 'politics'. They would fight between themselves, but also would come together for foreign wars under one Greek banner, each city providing its own army and leaders.

Tales from the earliest Greek history blend oral storytelling and myth, and so it is with the legendary King Minos of Crete. He was said to be the son of Zeus and Europa (see their story on page 31), and the leader of an ancient pre-Greek people now known as the Minoan civilization. Poseidon had helped Minos gain the powerful seat in Crete and sent him a beautiful white bull as his divine gift. When Minos refused to sacrifice the extraordinary beast in gratitude to the god, Poseidon took out revenge on Minos' wife, Pasiphaë, by making her fall in love with the bull.

She was so enamoured with the thing that she had a wooden cow construction made, which allowed her to climb inside and lure the attractive white bull to her. Her unorthodox plan worked, and she became pregnant by Poseidon's bull, eventually giving birth to a monstrous half-man half-bull, known as the Minotaur ('the Minoan bull').

Excavations in Crete found a sprawling palace in Knossos, dating from about 2200 BC. You can wander through much of the grounds and buildings today, and be amazed by the ancient paintings of athletes leaping over bulls. There is, however, no sign of the mythological labyrinth.

In the late 1800s, clay tablets unearthed at the Palace of Knossos revealed a previously unknown script of hieroglyphics, which was given the unimaginative name Linear B (because it was written in lines, and was the next such script to be found after one called Linear A). Thought to have been engraved as early as 1200 BC, these scripts were unintelligible even to Ancient Greek historians a few centuries later. It was a Phoenician alphabet from the eastern Mediterranean and beyond, and was made up of symbols and ideograms including simple spears, bulls' horns and stick figures. It wasn't until 1952 that they were finally deciphered by Michael Ventris at the University of Cambridge. He discovered that each of these symbols

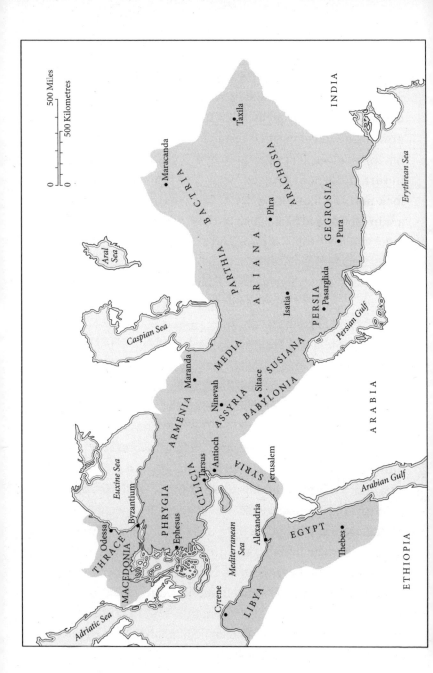

represented a syllable, similar to the Japanese script, and it was used as a rudimentary way to spell out Greek sounds using a non-Greek script. The Greek alphabet we know now didn't develop until around the eighth century BC, having evolved from the Linear B symbols. Greek script in turn influenced Roman script, and so our letters today look nothing like spears, bulls' horns or stick figures, but are in fact direct evolutions of them.

Alexander the Great

From 337 BC, Philip of Macedon managed to force many of the Greek states into submission, following centuries of wars and infighting, and he took control of Athens in Attica relatively peacefully. Philip invited delegates from most of the mainland states to Corinth, where they formed one union as Greeks under the Corinthian League, and promptly declared war on Persia. Philip was almost immediately assassinated, but his twenty-year-old son, Alexander III of Macedon, stepped straight into his shoes.

Within just a few years, Alexander had conquered the Persians in most of what is now Turkey, Israel and northern Egypt, where he founded the first of many cities he called Alexandria. The Egyptian one is still one of the country's largest cities today. He continued marching, and by 325 BC Alexander the Great had conquered an area reaching modern-day Iran, Afghanistan and Pakistan before making his way back towards Greece. Considering that the individual

Greek states had difficulties forming an alliance, it is utterly remarkable that he was able to make that alliance stretch so far that it touched India within just a matter of years. His spectacular achievement as a military leader was only limited by the dwindling of his men's fervour in continuing to march farther east away from home.

In 323 BC, Alexander caught a fever and died. The news tipped the balance of the fragile Athens, and the Corinthian Alliance once again descended into fighting. The result of this was a return to a more aristocratic rule with fewer democratic rights for the general population.

These early alliances between Greek states provided military and trading power beyond the size of any one state. The Delian League, based on the island of Delos from 477 BC, and Philip's Corinthian League are just two of these, and they enabled the Greek-speaking states to form large armies when faced with a common enemy, without necessarily having to totally surrender their own independence.

Greek Democracy

The word 'democracy' comes from the Greek *demos* ('the people') and *kratos* ('power'), and the system of civil law-making that they set up certainly was the start of people power running the country. Centuries of civil discord and aristocratic rule were most notably reformed in 508 BC, when politician Cleisthenes divided the Athenian state into ten regions known as *phylai*. Each of those regions was further divided into local *demes*, representing citizens from the towns, from the coast, and from rural areas. As such, each of the state's ten *phylai* sent a representative delegation of fifty citizens, who were chosen by lot to join the Assembly in Athens. This amassed a group of 500 men, who decided the agenda and laws to be discussed by an even wider group of up to six thousand eligible citizens.

The concept is admirable, and is a far cry from the aristocratic rule that most of humanity had known up until this point. It should be noted, however, that the ancient definition of democracy is not how we understand it today. The right to vote in Athens was only given to adult men with no criminal convictions, whose parents were both Athenian, so it is estimated that this may have given democratic rights to just 15 per cent of the population. While that sounds somewhat disempowering as a democratic system, it represents a pivotal moment in shaping human society, and it is truly astonishing that this level of voting rights wasn't achieved in the UK until two millennia later in the mid-nineteenth century.

This new age of civility heralds the start of the classical period of Greece's history, also known as its Golden Age. This is from around 500 BC to 300 BC, when much of its great literature, theatre, architecture, philosophy and science came into existence.

THE ROMAN KINGDOM

(753-510 BC)

Romulus

The ancient history of Rome's early days is likely to be more myth than fact, but the date of its very first ruler has been claimed as 753 BC under King Romulus. He was one of the famous twins, alongside his brother Remus, who were both suckled by a wolf and fed by a woodpecker before growing up to found the great city, and they were said to be the sons of war god Mars and a priestess, Rhea Silvia.

The twins disagreed about which hill to base the settlement on, and after one disrespectful act too many by Remus, Romulus murdered his brother and became the sole king of the city that he named after himself. During his reign, he expanded Rome from the original Palatine Hill across the neighbouring peaks. Across several centuries, Roman leaders would gain ground in all directions, eventually giving Rome the iconic Seven Hills that define the city to this day: adding the Capitoline, Quirinal, Viminal, Esquiline, Caelian and Aventine Hills.

King Romulus knew that any city of great power needed a large population and he was relentless in building up the numbers quickly, inviting passing criminals and slaves on the run into the city walls. But his tactic of appealing to an itinerant population meant that it was mainly men joining the inhabitants. The lack of women became not just apparent, but a challenge to the growth of the city if it wanted to survive longer than one generation.

Romulus held a huge festival and games dedicated to the sea god Neptune, and invited several regional populations to come and have a look at the fast-growing city that had recently appeared on the river Tiber, among them the local Sabine tribe. In the middle of the festivities, Romulus gave the signal to his ragtag clan, who at once grabbed all the young Sabine girls and fought off the Sabine men. It is a horrendous scene depicted in several pieces of Renaissance art as the rape of the Sabines. The young girls were forced to marry their captors, and the future of Rome was secured.

The Seven Kings of Rome

Following the rape of the Sabine women, Romulus' upstart city was attacked by several of the neighbouring tribes. Managing to defeat each one, Rome started its earliest colonization of land, grabbing whatever belonged to each conquered community. The fiercest war was with the Sabines themselves, and it was the greatest threat to Rome's survival, until a truce was called between the two tribes. They joined forces and the Sabine king, Titus Tatius, ruled together with Romulus over their combined population until his death. The compromise between them decreed that the kings of Rome would alternate between Roman and Sabine men, a tradition that remained in place for its first four kings. As Roman historians relayed, there was often an interregnum between kings, during which time the successor was being nominated and selected.

Where myth ends and actual history begins is disputed, but it's possible that most or all of Rome's seven kings existed as regional tribe leaders at some point during this period of Rome's emergence as a powerful city state. Progress that must have taken centuries is attributed to the actions of one man's rule. Legends and origin stories from a pre-Roman time could have been transposed onto the lives of those real tribal leaders to create a made-up, sequential history of the seven kings. The Romans of the classical age couldn't imagine anything other than Rome being powerful and important from day one, and so the narrative of an instant kingdom supports this worldview.

In this combining of myth and history, Rome's second king was the Sabine leader Numa Pompilius, who ruled from 715 to 673 BC. Numa is credited with a peaceful reign compared to that of the belligerent Romulus, and was recognized as bringing the worship of the gods Mars and Jupiter to the Roman people. It is said he established the Vestal Virgins, a tradition of very young girls chosen to hold the prestigious role of priestess for thirty years to safeguard the protection of Rome.

The third king was Tullus Hostilius, who reigned from 672 to 641 BC, and was said to be the grandson of a brave

Roman warrior who faced up to the Sabines during their earlier war with Romulus. As his name suggests (literally 'Tullus Hostile'), the peaceful times of Numa were over. He conquered the city of Alba Longa, leaving it utterly destroyed, but welcomed its leaders into the Roman Senate and brought its significant population under Roman rule.

The fourth mythical king of Rome was the Sabine leader Ancus Marcius, who is said to have ruled from 640 to 617 BC. He built the first ever bridge across the river Tiber, and he was the grandson of Numa Pompilius, Rome's second king. What is becoming clear of Rome's origins is that the society was already building on a perception of aristocracy, good family lineage and the succession of noble blood – values that remained ingrained in Rome for many centuries.

The fifth king was Tarquinius Priscus, who ruled from 616 to 578 BC. This is where struggles for power start to become prominent features of Roman history. Tarquinius was a guardian of the previous king's sons, but somehow found his own way to the throne rather than it going to Ancus Marcius' sons. As Tarquinius was of Greek heritage, his ascension to the throne also did away with the pact between the Romans and the Sabines to alternate kings from each people.

Ancus Marcius' sons eventually arranged for Tarquinius Priscus to be assassinated by an axe to the head during a staged riot in 578 BC. But the throne was not to be theirs, as Tarquinius' wife, Tanaquil, announced that the king had merely been wounded. Before the assassins could claim any right to the throne, she installed Servius Tullius – her son-in-law – into power. Already, the power struggles, assassinations and nepotism that we know of Rome's actual history is starting to creep into its mythology.

Servius Tullius ruled as Rome's sixth king from 578 to 535 BC. When Rome conquered the nearby town of Corniculum under the previous king, Ancus Marcius, a pregnant woman from that town was brought into the royal household as a slave to the king's wife, Tanaquil. The woman gave birth to Servius Tullus, who eventually married the king's daughter and was made king himself through Tanaquil's elaborate scheming.

Tullius is said to have introduced political systems and military organization into the kingdom, and to have been the first to use metal coins as currency. His reign came to an end when he was killed by his own daughter and her husband, Tarquinius Superbus – otherwise known as Tarquin the Proud.

Tarquin the Proud

Tarquinius Superbus – Tarquin the Proud – was the seventh and final king of Rome, ruling from 534 to 509 BC, and was the grandson of the fifth king, Tarquinius Priscus. The pride and arrogance associated with Tarquinius is epitomized by his unconventional rise from slave child to the throne, and he sought to cling to that power throughout his reign by whatever means necessary. He positioned himself as Rome's highest judge, and abused the power to remove his political rivals. His reign saw aggressive expansion of Roman territory, bringing the indigenous Latin people under Roman rule, overnight doubling its population and military.

Ruling with fear has its limit, and ultimately would lead to the downfall of the Roman monarchy. While Tarquinius was unsuccessfully attempting to conquer the Rutulians' city of Ardea, one of his sons back home raped the daughter of a Roman nobleman, Lucius Iunius Brutus. This goes down in legend as the trigger for aristocratic revolution, where the powerful men of Rome beat their own king in battle. Tarquinius fled, but spent the rest of his life trying to reclaim the throne. The monarchy was dead and the Roman Republic was born. It was finally free from its alliances with the various regional kings and could govern itself entirely independently.

It is thought that similar revolutions against monarchic rule were taking place all over southern Italy at the same time, and it's worth noting that this is around the same time that the first version of democracy was being introduced across the Athenian state of Attica in Greece by Cleisthenes (see page 82).

THE ROMAN REPUBLIC
(510-27 BC)

The Senate, Consuls and Dictators

E ven during the monarchy, Rome had the Senate, an advisory council to the king and senior noblemen of the city. At the birth of the Roman Republic, the Senate was an assembly of 300 aristocrats into which members were voted for a period of one year. They became the advisors to two consuls, a feature designed to prevent any one autocratic leader taking control as the kings had. This gave the system of governance a level of accountability not seen before, albeit just among the aristocracy. The word 'republic' comes from the Latin *res publica*, which means 'public matters': the affairs of the state had become – in principle at least – the responsibility of the people.

As ever with such utopian ideals, the dream didn't quite last. Already by 501 BC, it was decided that it might be beneficial to have one *dictator* in power, in case there was ever a situation that required one man's decisiveness. This introduction paved the way for the later emperors, who came after the Republic. It didn't take long for the position to get to people's heads, and between the years

444 and 366 BC, there were very few official consulship elections, and military leaders held those powers during this period instead.

To appreciate the influence of this very early system of government on the way we run countries today, you only need to look at the vocabulary of the US system, among others, in which senators, the Senate and even Washington's own Capitol Hill are lifted directly from the Roman set-up.

Rome developed a fiercely hierarchical society not dissimilar to the feudal system of medieval Europe. Aristocratic landowners defined themselves as *patricii* ('of the patrician class'), and they made the rules. The *plebes* would work beneath them, surviving on the agricultural yield of the small patches of land they could get their hands on, with many suffering through extortionate debts owed to the *patricii*. The class divide softened somewhat as some *plebes* became richer, with the first plebeian consul elected in 366 BC. The plebeian politics was nonetheless kept distanced from the politics governing the *patricii*.

Law of the Twelve Tables

As the plebeian population of Rome grew in influence, they demanded more fairness in trials and equality in the state. Their world had been run by the aristocratic *patricii*, and it was time for transparency and change. In 451 and 450 BC, the Roman Republic committed to a set of laws inscribed into twelve bronze tablets. From this moment on, there would be no disputing between right and wrong on certain topics, and the courts would be much fairer. The reality, however, was somewhat different, with the laws being defined by the *patricii* rather than the lower-class *plebes*, and therefore skewed in the interests of protecting the aristocracy.

From its very birth, Rome had idolized the literature, architecture, religion and culture of the Greeks, all of which would have been ancient and grand even to these Romans of the early Republic. And so it was with their laws: they sent a delegation of ten aristocrats over to Athens to study how the Greeks had implemented their own legal system nearly two hundred years beforehand. The Twelve Tables contained laws governing trial procedure, debt repayments, inheritance rights, land ownership rules, and rules of the patriarchy – a husband's ownership of his wife and children. Tables 11 and 12 were added a year after the original ten, prohibiting marriage between the social classes, and laying out the list of state-approved punishments, from flogging to being hurled off the side of the Capitoline Hill.

Over time, the Twelve Tables became gradually less relevant to the lives of average Romans, and by the first century BC were being talked about as a historical artefact rather than living law. The language was old-fashioned by that stage and they were no longer recited in schools as they had been before. Nonetheless, the model of writing clearly defined legislation to protect citizens, and doing so without reference to religion, became the cornerstone of sophisticated civilization. It is a practice that continues to be replicated in many nations to this day.

Julius Caesar

Julius Caesar is undoubtably the most well-known ruler of Rome. That's partly due to his gruesome assassination, partly due to the significant landgrabs he made for Rome, and partly due to the extensive memoirs he wrote of the wars he fought in Gaul, Hispania, Egypt and in Rome itself. It's amazing that we can still read his own thoughts during these wars, albeit in somewhat self-indulgent and self-aggrandizing versions of events.

The Death of Julius Caesar by Vincenzo Camuccini, *c.* 1805.

Born to a wealthy and politically influential family in 100 BC, Julius Caesar was always destined for a life in politics, but his journey there was by no means easy. As a young man, he was ousted and stripped of his wealth by the dictator Sulla, and had little choice but to join the army. He made a name for himself as a skilled soldier, rising through the ranks in both the military and eventually in the Republic itself, becoming the governor of Hispania (modern-day Spain). After Sulla's death, Caesar worked his way up to consul, effectively leading all of the Roman Republic alongside Pompey the Great and Crassus, Rome's wealthiest man. Despite his arrogant nature and wealthy upbringing, Caesar championed redistribution of land to the *plebes* and was artful in gaining following from soldiers and ordinary Roman citizens.

From 58 BC, Caesar spent nine years conquering and governing Gaul (modern-day France), invading Britain, and gaining considerable wealth in doing so. However, back in Rome, things weren't working in his favour. Crassus had been killed and Pompey was less aligned with Caesar's way of doing things. He was stripped of his governorship in Gaul and of his military position, and ordered to return to Rome. Caesar did so, but by marching his army in an act of defiance. When he crossed the river Rubicon, it marked the boundary between Gaul and Italy, and he effectively declared war on Rome itself. The phrase 'crossing the Rubicon' now refers to any act that marks a watershed moment, and one that cannot be undone.

Rather than defend Rome, Pompey fled to Egypt, but as

soon as he stepped off his boat, he was killed by order of the Egyptians, who had heard of Julius Caesar's de facto victory. Caesar was in hot pursuit behind Pompey, and created an immediate alliance with Cleopatra VII when he arrived in Egypt. She had been previously exiled, so the two of them took over the royal palace, where they remained under siege for six months (resulting in a son for Cleopatra) until Roman reinforcements arrived and ultimately defeated the Egyptian army.

> Victories on all sides of the Mediterranean cemented Caesar as one of the most successful military leaders that Rome had ever seen.

Back in Rome, Caesar was officially named the *dictator perpetuum* of the Republic in 44 BC – 'the dictator for life'. A common mistake is to call Caesar an emperor; the empire had not yet been invented and his title was that of a *dictator*, which held a similar meaning to the modern English word. The combination of Caesar's unchallenged power, his growing arrogance, and his disregard for Rome's moral standards led to increasing unease with the dictator. Three episodes are said to have been the catalysts for his assassination. The first came at a ceremony to honour Caesar with a number of titles. As the senators entered a temple to bestow the honours upon him, he refused to stand up to receive them, disrespecting their authority.

The second incident was when a diadem – an ornamental crown reserved only for the god Jupiter or for kings – was found on a statue of Caesar in the Roman Forum by two elected officials. Mere days later, the same officials arrested a member of the public who shouted out '*Rex!*' ('King!') to the dictator. Caesar had the two officials removed from office, angering not just political colleagues but the wider Roman population. The third episode occurred in front of a large crowd where Caesar was speaking during the Lupercalia festival. His co-consul Mark Antony presented Caesar with a diadem to wear. The crowd fell silent in disbelief, allowing Caesar to magnanimously refuse the offer three times. However, the incident was seen as a set-up by Caesar to test the crowd's reaction.

On the 15 March 44 BC – what the Romans called the Ides of March – Rome's senators met at the Theatre of Pompey in the centre of the city. Their usual meeting place in the Roman Forum was being renovated, so they met in this theatre complex. Caesar initially did not come to the meeting, heeding warnings from his wife's dream that he would be murdered on that day. One senator went to Caesar's home and convinced him to join the meeting. After he entered the room, gladiators from games being held at the venue blocked the door.

While discussing a piece of legislation, the sixty conspirators crowded round Caesar. At once, one senator held down the dictator. Another raised the first dagger and stabbed Caesar in the neck. A frenzied attack followed, with one dagger driving into his back, another into his face, another into his thigh, and more while Caesar crawled along the floor dying from the blood now gushing from him. In total he was stabbed twenty-three times as the other members of the Senate fled in horror. His final words are contested, but are often quoted as his disbelief in seeing his friend and heir, Brutus, among the conspirators: *'Et tu, Brute?'* ('Even you, Brutus?'). The Roman historian Suetonius quotes a far more heartrending version of this, with Caesar uttering the Greek phrase 'καὶ σύ, τέκνον' (*'Kai su, teknon?'*), meaning 'Even you, my boy?'

The site of Caesar's assassination is visible in Rome today, in an unassuming ruin surrounded by a busy junction of roads, and overrun by a population of stray cats. It is easy to completely overlook one of the most important locations and emotional moments in Rome's history. Following his death, the month of Quintilis, dedicated to Rome's founding father Romulus, was renamed July in honour of Julius Caesar.

Mark Antony

Mark Antony was a cousin of Julius Caesar and held significant positions in his inner circle, in both the military and in politics. He was an asset to Caesar's conquest of Gaul, although his boozing and fraternizing with the regular soldiers gained him more appeal with them rather than with the ruling aristocracy of Rome. After Caesar's assassination, Mark Antony spoke at his funeral in favour of the dictator, in an address memorialized in Shakespeare's play *Julius Caesar* as the 'Friends, Romans, countrymen' speech.

Despite Mark Antony's desire to step into Caesar's shoes and lead the Republic, he faced competition from Caesar's great nephew and adopted son, the nineteen-year-old Octavian. A power struggle took place and their armies fought in Gaul against one another, but ultimately an agreement was made. Octavian ruled the west of the Republic, based in Rome, while Mark Antony ruled the east, from Tarsus in modern-day Turkey. A third leader, Lepidus, ruled over northern Africa. Together, they defeated the armies of two of Julius Caesar's assassins, Brutus and Cassius.

In his new position in the east of the Republic, Antony summoned Caesar's mistress, Cleopatra VII of Egypt, with a view to charging her with helping the conspirators. However, Cleopatra had no intention of playing along. She arrived in Tarsus, where Antony was stationed, on a barge extravagantly decorated with purple sails and silver oars. Flutes and harps played around her, as she lay regally under a golden canopy, being fanned by beautiful boys. Rather than appear before his makeshift court, she invited him for an opulent dinner surrounded by trees festooned with decorations in beautiful candlelight. A romance for the ages was born.

At the same time, Antony's relationship with Octavian deteriorated. Several attempts to stop the affair with Cleopatra failed, including marrying Antony to Octavian's sister. Knowing there was still some support for the disgraced leader in the Roman Senate, Octavian convinced them to declare war against Cleopatra alone. The Battle of Actium in 31 BC was the culmination of that war, with a sea battle that saw Antony defeated.

In the Roman Forum was a Temple of Jupiter. Its two opposing doors remained open at all times. It was said that the doors would only be closed when there was peace across the whole Roman world. They had only been closed twice from the age of Romulus, until Octavian closed them for the third time in 700 years after defeating Mark Antony at the Battle of Actium.

Antony stabbed himself upon hearing that Cleopatra had died following the battle, but the rumour wasn't true, and he ended up being brought to her and dying in her arms. Inconsolable, she took her own life by swallowing a poison. Her son by Julius Caesar was strangled to death at Octavian's order, while her eldest by Mark Antony was also killed, and the younger ones were brought up in Rome.

THE ROMAN EMPIRE
(27 BC–AD 476)

Augustus Caesar

After the defeat of Mark Antony at the Battle of Actium, Octavian was finally the sole ruler of Rome. In 27 BC, he was given the title Augustus, meaning 'sacred' or 'grand', and became the very first emperor of a new phase for the civilization: the Roman Empire. The titles bestowed on him by a devoted Senate increased in adoration and power during his rule. He first held the position of *imperator* (from where we get the English word 'emperor'), then was declared *imperium maius* ('supreme emperor') in 19 BC, and later *pater patriae* ('father of our country') in 2 BC. The month of August was named in his honour during this time, and he ruled until his death at the age of seventy-five.

Following decades of unrest, war and civil wars since the death of Julius Caesar, Augustus knew that he had to act as a stabilizing force for the Roman people if he was to have any success as a leader. He is recognized simultaneously as a ruler who made some of the most significant land expansions of the Roman world, as well as a bringer of peace. He managed this by declaring all the lands and people he annexed as being at peace. Once they had been conquered by the almighty Roman army, they were at once Roman, and so no longer at war. This neat paradox was given a propaganda-friendly name of *Pax Romana* ('Roman Peace'), in the same way that modern wars are sometimes waged in the name of enforcing 'democracy' on countries that don't necessarily seem to want it.

By the end of his reign, Augustus had expanded the Roman Empire to cover the whole of the Mediterranean. All of modern-day Portugal, Spain, France, Switzerland, Italy and Greece were under Roman rule. The empire stretched into areas of modern-day Belgium, Germany, Austria, Ukraine, Turkey, Israel, Egypt, Tunisia and Algeria. The wealth, slaves and trade that flowed into Rome made this period the golden age of the civilization, with significant advancements in architecture and technology, including aqueducts and public baths.

Augustus Caesar cemented his ideals of the Roman Empire by commissioning the poet Virgil to compose a new origin story for Rome, in the *Aeneid*. He died in AD 14, uttering the words '*marmoream se relinquere, quam latericiam accepisset*': 'I found a city of clay bricks, and have left a city of marble.'

Caligula

Augustus Caesar was succeeded by his stepson Tiberius, who remained constantly fearful of being overthrown and did away with political rivals wherever he could. One such perceived threat came from a wealthy woman within the family dynasty called Agrippina, who had ambitions for her sons to reach the top of the Roman Empire. Tiberius banished her and her eldest son, but kept the daughters and the youngest boy, Caligula, under his watch. This boy was the great-grandson of Augustus Caesar on his mother's side, and the great-grandson of Mark Antony on his father's side, but was never deemed a threat to Tiberius' power.

Alongside his sisters, Caligula was brought to the island of Capri at the age of nineteen as a prisoner of Emperor Tiberius. He treated his captor with obsequious reverence, and seemed to enjoy observing first-hand the tortures and executions that took place on Tiberius' orders. When Tiberius died, Caligula rose to emperor in AD 37, and was initially very popular in the role. He cancelled a raft of treason trials, welcomed back exiles into the city, and made popular infrastructure and architectural additions to the Roman world.

However, something shifted in Caligula after just a few months in office. He became suspicious and excessive; he raised the taxes he had previously reduced; and one historian notes how excited and bloodthirsty the emperor seemed at the brutal gladiatorial games. At one point, he suggested he would nominate his horse as a consul of the empire, and he was outraged that the Jewish people in Judea wouldn't worship him as a god.

Caligula hadn't even reached four years as emperor when he was murdered by his own guards in AD 41, alongside his wife and daughter. He was succeeded by his uncle Claudius, the only remaining adult male in the family.

Nero

After Claudius' reign came Emperor Nero, born the son of one of Caligula's sisters, Agrippina the Younger. She was as ambitious as the rest of what is known as the Julio-Claudian

A statue relief of Emperor Nero on the gateway entrance to the park that contains the ruins of his golden palace in Rome.

dynasty. When Claudius became available, she married him and saw that he adopted her son Nero in order to secure his lineage. Claudius died suddenly, following a suspected poisoning from mushrooms, rumoured to be Agrippina's doing. Nero came to power in AD 54 at the age of just sixteen (favoured over Claudius' son by birth, Britannicus), with Agrippina very much pulling the strings in the background of his chaotic reign.

Much like Caligula, Nero was a well-liked leader to start with. He was young blood in the seat of power, and brought about popular reforms to hand back some powers to the Senate, while sponsoring a series of gladiatorial games and festivals and throwing himself into the culture of Rome. He was a keen singer and lyre player, and his audiences were prohibited from leaving during his many and lengthy recitals, despite his reputed lack of ability.

Agrippina's constant involvement in his rule soon began to grate, and Nero started to distance himself from his mother, moving her out of the palace, removing her state protection and banning her from public games. In retaliation, she formed a closer bond with Nero's stepbrother, Britannicus, and the two became a threat to Nero's position. It wasn't long before Britannicus became the victim of yet another mysterious poisoning, and Agrippina became the focus of Nero's next murder. He first had engineers shipped in from Egypt build an elaborate contraption designed to crush her as she lay in her bed. When that failed, he had a sinkable ship built in order to claim an accidental drowning, but Agrippina was able to swim to shore after the sinking. Finally, he did away with convoluted plots and had her decisively stabbed.

Nero's murderous streak didn't stop there. His first wife, Octavia, was banished for alleged adultery and then made to look like she had died by suicide. That allowed Nero to marry his mistress, the married and pregnant Poppaea Sabina. Their first child sadly died, and the second one was killed when Nero kicked Poppaea in the belly during her pregnancy. She also died from those injuries.

Things weren't looking good for Nero politically either. There was an assassination plot by his own senators, leading to forty-one executions, and unrest across the empire provided a challenge to his leadership. The final straw came in the form of a massive fire that destroyed huge swathes of central Rome in AD 64, leaving thousands without a home. Nero used the opportunity of cleared land to build the most ostentatious palace at one end of the Roman Forum, leading some to ask whether he had started the fire himself.

Nero's misguided love of music and singing led to the origination of the English phrase 'to fiddle while Rome burns' – not giving due attention when something is going wrong. Fiddles weren't invented at this point, but the sentiment is that the extravagant emperor strummed his lyre in his palace while most of the city burned for six days.

Nero's spiralling chaos saw him marry a young Greek slave boy in AD 67, whom he had castrated and play the role of empress, stating that he reminded him so much of his murdered wife, Poppaea. The various excesses and lawlessness finally led to Nero being declared an enemy of the state and replaced as emperor by Galba in AD 68. That marked the end of the incredible Julio-Claudian dynasty that had ruled since Augustus Caesar became the first emperor of Rome in 27 BC. In exile, Nero died by suicide or assisted suicide, uttering the words, *'qualis artifex pereo!'* – 'What an artist dies in me!'

The Year of the Four Emperors

Any Roman citizen wanting a more peaceful time following Nero's death was not in luck, as AD 69 brought with it civil wars and four emperors. Nero's replacement, Emperor Galba, was gone by January of that year, after just eight months in power, when he was murdered by his own guards at the instruction of Marcus Otho. Otho succeeded him, but was also out very quickly. The Roman Empire had become huge and difficult to govern, and there was unrest in the powerful military legions in Germania and Asia Minor. The Germanic legion put its support behind their governor Vitellius, while the legions in Egypt, Judea and Syria favoured Vespasian as their leader.

In March of AD 69, Vitellius amassed several armies of allies and they marched down into northern Italy. They were met by Otho's armies and up to forty thousand soldiers lost their lives in the Battle of Bedriacum that took place in April. It became clear that Otho could not win, and he committed suicide rather than be responsible for any further deaths. Vitellius marched down to Rome and was declared the year's third emperor so far.

However, Vitellius' style of leadership soon became cause for alarm. He nearly bankrupted the treasury with a series of lavish banquets, parades and festivals, and thought little of executing political rivals or those who called in their debts from the extravagant emperor. Meanwhile, Vespasian was gathering support from across Asia Minor and launched his own armies into Italy, defeating Vitellius' soldiers in a second Battle of Bedriacum. Eventually, they reached the gates of Rome, and a bloody battle took place on the city's streets. Up to fifty thousand people lost their lives in protecting the city against Vespasian's army, but the victory was his in the end. His supporters dragged Vitellius out into the near-destroyed streets, where he was brutally murdered. His body was thrown into the Tiber and his head was paraded through the city. Vespasian was declared emperor in December of AD 69, heralding the start of the Flavian dynasty.

The chaos of AD 69 was in part caused by the lack of clarity of succession rules in Rome. The members of the Julio-Claudian dynasty that preceded it equally had to resort to murder and conspiracy to jostle their way into the seat of power, but they at least had some claim to the position by keeping it in the family. This wouldn't be the last time that Rome would see such political upheaval, with the Year of Five Emperors in AD 193 and the splitting of Rome into the Eastern and Western Empires in the third century AD.

The Flavian Dynasty

The Flavian dynasty is the name given to three related emperors – Vespasian, Titus and Domitian – who ruled from AD 69 to AD 96. Following the excesses of Nero, the cost of several civil wars, and the mismanagement of the treasury by Vitellius particularly, Emperor Vespasian knew that he had work to do to bring not just calm to the Roman Empire, but financial security as well. He claimed that his mission was first to stabilize the empire, then to adorn it. He raised taxes, increased revenues from across the empire, reclaimed disused land in Italy, and controlled spending. He filled in what remained of Nero's outrageous Golden House and began work on a building for the people in its place: the almighty Colosseum, funded by Vespasian's siege and destruction of Jerusalem.

Vespasian died of natural causes in AD 79 – something that hadn't happened to an emperor in over sixty years – and had already declared his sons as his heir, Titus followed by Domitian. In doing so, he ensured the stability of the Roman Empire compared with the disorder that had preceded the Flavian dynasty.

Titus reigned for just two years until AD 81, but

nonetheless played an influential part in Rome's history. He was recognized for his compassion and action at the eruption of Mount Vesuvius in AD 79, which destroyed – and preserved – the city of Pompeii. He oversaw the completion of the Colosseum and held its opening games, during which over nine thousand animals were slaughtered in front of a cheering crowd of up to eighty thousand daily spectators. The Flavians were aware that they had no claim of heritage to the position of emperor, so they were

Exotic wild animals were brought from the far reaches of the Roman Empire and used in hunts at the Colosseum.

keen to make bold statements that gathered support and popularity. Nothing did this better than the construction of one of the world's biggest arenas – even to this day – and all the celebration that came with gladiatorial contests. Gladiators were the ultimate celebrities of their day, with ardent followers who idolized their favourite fighters, graffitied their names and images on walls and bought their merchandise.

Domitian took over as emperor when Titus died of natural causes, and he immediately deified his brother – the start of a tradition that turned emperors into gods and gave them much more cultural significance than simply being political leaders. His reign was more tyrannical than his brother's and father's, and he removed much of the power from the Senate. During his reign, further advances were made into Britannia, up to modern-day Scotland, as well as into Asia Minor, reaching modern-day Azerbaijan. However, his autocratic rule eventually came to an end in AD 96, when he was assassinated by his close attendants, in a conspiracy masterminded by court officials.

That marked the end of the Flavian dynasty, whose legacy is in restoring stability and financial security to Rome, and in building some of its most iconic buildings.

The Fall of the Roman Empire

It is hard to imagine how the Roman Empire ever ceased to exist, with such rich civilization and influence that spanned a huge section of the world. There are a number of factors that contributed to its gradual disintegration over a long period of time. It is in fact in large part due to its size that the empire became ever harder to govern, to defend militarily, to fund and to maintain as one coherent concept.

In the second century AD, Emperor Trajan led a period of massive growth of the empire, extending Roman influence across the whole of the Mediterranean on all sides, ruling an area that covered modern-day Italy, Spain, Greece, Israel, Egypt, northern Africa, parts of Saudi Arabia, Iraq, Iran, southern Europe, France and England. He also continued the great advancement in construction and architecture across his large empire. Such growth caused inevitable problems with governance, and towards the end of the third century AD, Emperor Diocletian split the empire into two administrative regions, the Eastern and Western Empires, eventually creating two equal *Augustus* leaders that were each supported by a junior *Caesar*. It is perhaps the presence of too many simultaneous leaders that meant this model was short-lived. By AD 306, Constantine had united the whole empire again, albeit amid a series of civil wars. It is around this time that Christianity began gradually to overtake the old polytheistic religion of Rome, creating yet more fractures and civil war in the fragile empire.

By the fifth century AD, the notions of Eastern and Western Empires were still strong, and leadership was governed more by military leaders than by more democratic emperors. The Western Empire came under attack by

Germanic armies from the north, and in AD 476 the emperor Romulus Augustus couldn't rely solely on the heritage of his given name and was overthrown by the Germanic leader Odacer. This moment is seen as the end of the Western Roman Empire based in Rome, but the Eastern Roman Empire continued to thrive.

The extraordinary growth of the empire meant that it had enveloped many different nations and cultures, and it is thought that by the time of the Germanic victory in AD 476, the people of the empire had lost the central vein of Roman sentiment that was responsible for its initial success. The citizens of the Eastern Empire managed to retain pride in a Roman identity for many centuries longer. It continued to assert its might across the Mediterranean, but was centred around the city of Constantinople (modern-day Istanbul) and Greece. Greek was reinstated as the official language of the empire in the seventh century AD, although the Roman identity remained strong. Constantinople eventually fell in an attack from Western European Catholics in AD 1206, but it was rebuilt, and the idea of the Roman Empire kept going until AD 1453, when it was finally consumed by the Ottoman Empire.

CHAPTER 4

WARS

GREEK WARS

The Trojan War

The Trojan War is undoubtably the most influential struggle of both the Ancient Greek and Ancient Roman worlds. It is a story of legend that acts as the backdrop to so much of classical literature, tragedy and mythology that its key players are still household names around the world today. Achilles fights for the Greeks on the plains outside the city walls; Roman hero Aeneas defends the city as a Trojan leader from within the walls; Odysseus encounters the Cyclops and countless other monsters on his long journey home from the war; the Trojan Horse gives the Greeks their stealthy way into the city; King Agamemnon sacrifices his own daughter to help the Greeks reach Troy and is murdered by his wife Clytemnestra on his return to Mycenae many years later. There seem to be very few mythological tales that are not in some way touched by the events that took place in this one city.

Classical Greeks believed the legends to be based on a real, historical event: a ten-year war that took place in the twelfth or thirteenth century BC. Whether it ever occurred – and even whether Troy existed at all – remained a matter of debate until the excavation in the 1850s of an ancient city on the Turkish coast seemed to accord with descriptions of Troy.

With such a cataclysmic clash as this, it should come as no surprise that the war starts with the gods. Olympian brothers Zeus and Poseidon are both smitten with a sea-nymph called Thetis and they compete for her affections. But they are warned by a prophecy that she will bear a son more powerful than any of the gods if they proceed, and so Zeus decrees that she will marry a mortal, King Peleus of Phthia. A huge festival is held to celebrate their marriage, with all the gods in attendance apart from one: Zeus' daughter Eris, whose very name means 'Discord'.

Not to have her presence ignored, Eris lives up to her name by throwing a golden apple into the middle of the godly crowd. Upon it is one word: καλλίστῃ (*kallistei*), 'for the prettiest one'. It instigates an argument between three goddesses, who claim the apple should be theirs: Hera, the wife of Zeus; Athena, goddess of wisdom; and Aphrodite, the goddess of love. Zeus sends them to the prince of Troy,

The legendary Trojan Horse.

Paris, to make the impossible judgement. Hera promises him power over Europe and Asia, and Athena offers him the wisdom that she oversees. But it is Aphrodite's offer of the world's most beautiful woman, Queen Helen of Sparta, that wins the golden apple.

Unfortunately, Helen's hand in marriage is not Aphrodite's to give, as the queen is already married to King Menelaus. While the king is away, Aphrodite disguises Paris as a messenger on a diplomatic mission to Sparta, and arms him with one of the potent love arrows from her son Eros. Helen instantly falls in love with Paris and is abducted to Troy. This is the trigger for war, and Menelaus gathers armies from allies across the whole of Greece.

One Greek king and noted warrior that he is keen to recruit is Odysseus. However, having just married and had a young son, King Odysseus of Ithaca has other plans in mind. He is also mindful of the tragic prophecy that, if he were to lead an army to Troy, it would take him many years to return home. To discourage the delegation that has come to recruit him, Odysseus pretends to have lost his mind. He ties a plough to a donkey and an ox, and starts sowing salt granules in a field. Unconvinced by this act, one delegate places Odysseus' young son, Telemachus, in the path of the plough. Odysseus is forced to divert its course and admit that he has all of his faculties. He commits to joining the allied Greek armies with his own fleet of twelve ships, and makes one of the most important decisions of the war: recruiting the son of Peleus and Thetis, the great hero Achilles, to the army. No other single person has more of an impact on the ultimate Greek victory than he does.

The legend of the Trojan War initiates three of the most important works of the ancient world: the epic poems of Homer and Virgil. Homer's poem the *Iliad*, composed in the eighth century BC, tells the story of the Greek siege of the walled city, with the work named after Troy's second name, Ilium. His subsequent poem the *Odyssey* tells of that one warrior's troubled journey home, adding ten years to his time away from his wife and young family.

These tales were ancient legend even for classical Greeks who studied them many hundreds of years later. And when the Roman Empire was formed in the first century BC, its first emperor commissioned Rome's own imitations of those prehistoric works in Virgil's Latin poem the *Aeneid*. That tells of a Trojan leader who has to leave the destroyed city to travel across the Mediterranean to found the future city of Rome.

The Persian Wars

In the period from 492 to 449 BC, there was a series of wars in which Persian armies unsuccessfully tried to conquer Greece. The coalescing of Greek resources and armies against this enemy helped solidify the strength of the region and led to the formation of the Delian League. Named after its base on the island of Delos, it was a formal alliance of several Greek states, giving them much more military, financial and political power than any individual state could expect before the Persian Wars took place.

The first attack was made under Persian leader Darius. At this time, the Persian Empire was hugely influential, covering a vast area of the Middle East and Asia, including modern-day Turkey and some of the Greek islands and mainland states. When the states of Athens and Sparta joined forces to shore up their military strength, Darius sent a fleet of 600 ships to make further landgrabs in the Greek islands, approaching ever closer to the seat of Athens.

One of the great clashes was the Battle of Marathon in 490 BC, where 90,000 Persian soldiers faced a Greek army of just 15,000 men. Despite a torrent of Persian arrows, the Greeks' superior armour and more sophisticated strategy saw them victorious. They arranged themselves into phalanx formations: tightly structured groups of soldiers known as hoplites, who were protected on all sides by large bronze shields. The hoplites' huge spears made direct contact difficult, and their swords would greet you if you made it through. In combat, the phalanx would spread out to envelop the line of enemy soldiers before them.

As the Persian army was defeated and started their retreat, one ship seemed to be diverting its course directly towards Athens. To avoid it attacking Athens or claiming a false victory in the battle, it was important to get the message to the city that the Persians had been defeated. That task was given to the messenger Pheidippides, who ran history's first marathon – named after the site of the battle – all the way to Athens to deliver the news. He threw away his armour and eventually his clothes to make the heroic journey as quickly as possible. Taking a route round Mount Pentelicus, he is said to have covered a distance of about 40 kilometres (around 25 miles) before rushing into the Athenian assembly to announce: 'We have won!' At that moment, the legend goes that he dropped to the floor and died.

The Peloponnesian War

The legacy of the Persian Wars was to unite over three hundred Greek city states under one alliance known as the Delian League, named after its base on the island of Delos. The biggest players were Sparta, Corinth and Athens, the city that had always held a powerful position in Greece. Athens was already receiving revenues from various Greek states and dependants as the head of the Delian League, and had a powerful and experienced navy. While Athens excelled at sea, Sparta had a more skilled land army. In 454 BC, even while the latter stages of various battles against the Persians were continuing, Athenian general Pericles moved the Delian League's treasury from Delos to his own city. It was seen as an affront to the authority of Sparta and Corinth, as Athens started enriching its own coffers from Delian profits. So, even though the unity of Greek states had been the reason for an eventual victory over the Persians, it could not stop them fighting between themselves for ultimate control of the Greek world.

The First Peloponnesian War took place in 460–446 BC, mainly between Athens and Corinth, supported by Sparta.

The name refers to the huge peninsula that is the southern landmass of mainland Greece, and the location of both Sparta and Corinth. Athens was eventually victorious, having encircled the Peloponnesian peninsula and cut off their access via the mainland. There came a few years of relative peace, following a truce with the Persians and no all-out war between the Greek states. But the divisions were never truly gone, and the Peloponnesian War kicked off again in earnest in 431 BC.

Athens had once again exerted its authority over other Greek states by laying siege to the city of Poteidaia until it handed over its timber and resources, and by enforcing a trade embargo on the city of Megara. Both places were important allies and trading partners of Corinth, and it just took a few small sparks of fighting to ignite all-out war once more. The Second Peloponnesian War continued until 404 BC and saw new advancements in war strategy and sophistication. The phalanxes of hoplite soldiers that had proved so successful against the Persians became wider and deeper in the number of soldiers who marched into combat together, and they were joined by more nimble foot soldiers and charging cavalry on horseback.

The war was typified by taking cities by siege: surrounding the city walls until its trapped inhabitants either starved to death or were driven to infighting. Such conquests could take months or even years to be victorious, and so further developments were made in battering rams to break down walls, and in the defences against such attacks. In the nearly thirty years of battle on land and at sea, some members of the disintegrating Delian League started defecting to Sparta, as did one of Athens' key generals, Alcibiades. Even the Persians started courting – and financing – the Spartans when they saw how weakened the Greek world had become.

It was this final intervention that allowed Sparta to build a fleet of 200 ships and beat the mighty Athenian navy at Aegospotami in 405 BC. Peace was declared the following year, with Sparta taking control of the Greek world and Athens thoroughly weakened in power and military might.

A Pyrrhic Victory

The Pyrrhic War refers to the battles fought by King Pyrrhus of Epirus, a Greek state in modern-day north-west Greece and Montenegro, in 280–275 BC. At this time, the Roman Republic was expanding well beyond the city of Rome and was making headway across the Italian peninsula. The southern area of present-day Puglia – the heel of Italy's boot – was still part of Greece, and the region sought help from Pyrrhus against the advancing Romans.

Pyrrhus left in haste for the city of Tarentum with 25,000 soldiers and 20 military elephants – a sight the Roman legions were not used to facing. Sailing in winter, however, they faced a choppy and stormy Adriatic Sea. Several ships ended up wrecked, or diverted to Sicily and even northern Africa. Pyrrhus himself only reached Tarentum by jumping overboard and swimming to the shore. Perhaps this was a sign of things to come for his army.

Undeterred, Pyrrhus made his presence in Tarentum felt, turning the city into something of a military state with strict rules on social gatherings and enforced military service. Significant battles against the Roman Republic saw losses and victories on both sides, and drove the Romans to find an ally in Carthage, in present-day Tunisia. In 278 BC, Pyrrhus turned his attentions to fighting the Carthaginians on the island of Sicily, and back on the mainland against the Romans in 275 BC, with his elephants and a depleted number of soldiers in tow. It was a final battle at Beneventum that would see the end of Pyrrhus' war. His army got lost in the thick forest in their approach to the town, trudging all night through muddy and overgrown passes. When dawn came, they were exhausted and demoralized, and their approach was in full view of the awaiting Roman army.

The one thing that had made Pyrrhus' army unique – its small contingent of elephants – became its downfall. A single spear hurled into an elephant calf caused a stampede through the ranks of Pyrrhus' own men, and in the ensuing chaos the Romans gained the upper hand and were victorious.

It is from one of Pyrrhus' earlier victories against the Romans that we get the phrase 'Pyrrhic victory', referring to a win in any situation that has caused as much damage to the victor as to the defeated.

ROMAN WARS

The Punic Wars

The Punic Wars were a series of three wars fought between the Roman Republic and the Carthaginians between 264 and 146 BC. The Carthaginians, based in modern-day Tunisia, were also known as the Punic civilization, from a Latin word linked to their 'Phoenician' heritage. The Roman Republic was making significant headway in controlling most of the Italian peninsula following their defeat of Pyrrhus and the Greeks in 275 BC. However, this left the strategically situated island of Sicily as a chink in their armour. If any powerful empire gained control of such a large province, it would put them in an advantageous position to invade Roman land.

The Carthaginians, meanwhile, absolutely had their eyes on Sicily, to add to their strategic outposts dotted around the large islands of the Mediterranean. They had already fought Pyrrhus here just a few years earlier and were keen to expand their influence on the island. When a gang of mercenaries took over Messana, one of Sicily's most important port cities, the Sicilians asked both Carthage and Rome to come to their aid. The Carthaginians were first on the scene and occupied the town, seemingly in the interests of restoring order. The Romans arrived shortly

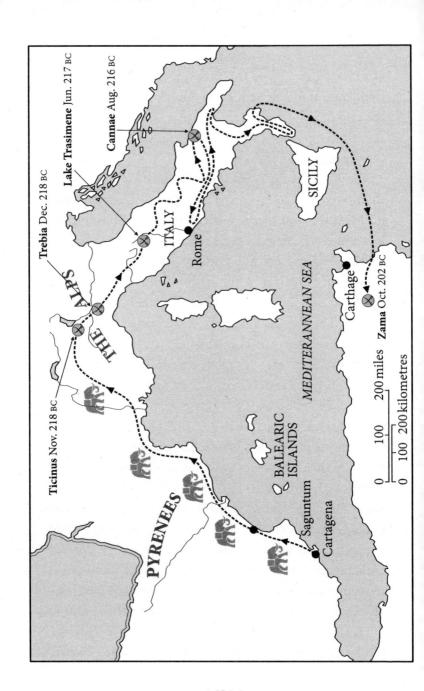

Trebia Dec. 218 BC

Lake Trasimene Jun. 217 BC

Cannae Aug. 216 BC

Ticinus Nov. 218 BC

THE ALPS

ITALY

Rome

PYRENEES

Saguntum

Cartagena

BALEARIC ISLANDS

MEDITERANNEAN SEA

SICILY

Carthage

Zama Oct. 202 BC

0   100   200 miles

0   100   200 kilometres

afterwards and filled the relatively peaceful town with their own soldiers. Tensions were already high between the two superpowers, and war broke out after an argument seemingly got out of hand and the Romans seized the Carthaginian general.

The First Punic War raged on land and sea for more than twenty years from 264 to 241 BC. It initially centred on Messana and Sicily, but the Romans diverted their attentions to Carthaginian outposts in Corsica, and then established one of their own on Carthaginian land in the city of Clypea. This was a significant moment for the Romans, and they were able to come close to declaring all-out victory following both naval and territorial wins against the less organized Carthaginians. They once again began serious attacks in Sicily, and ultimately claimed full control of the island, bringing the war to an end in 241 BC.

Over the following two decades, the Romans flaunted their expanding power in the Mediterranean, and the Carthaginians were left to lick their wounds. In pursuit of restoring their finances and influence, they sent one general, Hamilcar, over to Spain to expand the Carthaginian presence there. One of his sons, Hannibal, became an accomplished military leader with a lifelong vendetta against the Roman Republic. When Hannibal advanced on the Hispanic town of Saguntum, it was seen as a step too far away from the restrictions placed on Carthage following the previous war. The Second Punic War ensued and ran from 218 to 201 BC.

Hannibal knew that the Roman fleet was too powerful for the Carthaginians to defeat, as it created an impenetrable barrier around the whole Italian peninsula. The only way he could see to sow discord in the Roman people was to enter overland and bring war onto Roman territory. He and his army began the arduous journey from modern-day southern Spain, fighting Hispanics and Gauls along the way, and recruiting others to join him. He crossed the Alps with around forty-five thousand men and thirty-eight elephants, in what must have been an extraordinary sight for the mountain villages and cattle herders. It is not thought that many of the animals survived the arduous trek across the cold mountain range. Hannibal had a decisive victory at the Battle of Cannae, and even claimed land in southern Italy. Ultimately, though, the Romans were victorious again and Hannibal fled to Carthage.

While land ownership struggles continued in Sicily, Italy and Hispania, there was a fifty-year gap until the Third Punic War. During this interlude, Carthage had regained a small part of its wealth through trade and was starting to grab the attention of the Roman Senate once again. Instigated by a senator now known as Cato the Elder, the Romans sent an army over to Carthage and made absurd demands that they cease trading and move inland away from the port. The war that ensued from 149 to 146 BC – relatively short compared to previous clashes – was essentially a protracted siege of the city of Carthage. Led by general Scipio, the Romans blocked the Carthaginian's access by land and even built a causeway to prevent them accessing supplies by sea. They cut off the city's trade, and launched endless attacks on its people. They eventually breached the city walls and advanced street by street, slaughtering 80 per cent of its population.

The Romans gained power over not just Carthage and its now-enslaved people, but also over a huge proportion of the Mediterranean and northern coast of the African continent.

Caesar's Civil War

There are few military leaders in ancient history who have left us with more personal accounts of their campaigns than Julius Caesar. His military diaries – which he knew were for public publishing – were mainly written before he came the dictator of the Roman Republic, and give a first-hand account of his conquest of Gaul, and of his civil war against his own political rivals. They are pompous, one-sided accounts that are perfect propaganda for his rise to power, but they nonetheless give a unique insight into the battles that took place. At any rate, they at least let us step into Caesar's thoughts of what he wanted Roman citizens to think of him. He was an accomplished orator and writer, and it is from his works that we get the phrase *'veni, vidi, vici'*: 'I came, I saw, I conquered.'

The triggers for a civil war started when Caesar was the governor of Gaul. He had conquered that land and made attempts on Britannia, and was one of the top leaders of the Roman Republic through an informal alliance known the First Triumvirate ('three-man leadership'). Alongside Rome's richest man, Crassus, and his co-consul, Pompey, the three men assured each other's prolonged positions of power. Caesar effectively ruled Gaul, while Pompey controlled Hispania and Crassus held the same power in Syria.

Crassus was defeated and killed in battle and the relationship between Caesar and Pompey disintegrated. Knowing that he would be stripped of his position in Gaul, Caesar set his sights on the top job: the consul of the Roman Republic. However, he feared the transition from one job to the next. If he found himself caught in the no-man's land between military leader and political leader for even a short period, it was certain his rivals and adversaries would come for him with a raft of criminal charges, against which he would not have the protection he had so far enjoyed. Several attempts were made in the Senate to remove Caesar from his position, which he was able to hold off for a while with plebeian accomplices arguing and voting in his favour.

In December of 50 BC, the politician Marcellus reached agreement with the Senate that both Caesar and his rival Pompey were to relinquish their military posts of Gaul and Hispania simultaneously, thereby giving some assurance that one would not go after the other. However, Marcellus also went behind the Senate's back to offer Pompey control over legions in Italy. Caesar did not give up his control of the Gallic army either, and marched them across the tiny river Rubicon in northern Italy. As the formal dividing line between Gaul and Italy, that otherwise inconsequential river crossing became a declaration of war against Pompey and the Republic itself.

The Battle of Actium

The Battle of Actium marked the end of Rome's last power struggle for many years. Mark Antony had succeeded Julius Caesar as the dictator of the Roman Republic, but Caesar's great nephew – and adopted son – Octavian also laid claim to the top job. In 43 BC, the two men, alongside another called Lepidus, created the Second Triumvirate – the 'three-man leadership'. They became co-dictators, each with a part of the Roman world to govern, while sharing control of Italy itself. They had success as an alliance in defeating the armies of Brutus and Cassius, two of Julius Caesar's assassins, who had gathered considerable following and influence in the east of the Roman Republic.

However, the rivalry remained particularly strong between Mark Antony and Octavian, and was to lead to the disintegration of the Triumvirate and the death of one of them. Lepidus tried to take control of Sicily by force, and so was made to resign from his position, while Mark Antony formed a scandalous union with the Egyptian Queen Cleopatra VII from his outpost in modern-day Turkey. This left Octavian with free rein in Rome itself, and he made it his mission to ensure that he became the sole leader of the entire Republic.

The trigger for turning from animosity to war came after Mark Antony had invaded Parthia unsuccessfully in 35 BC and Armenia – successfully – the following year, both with financial backing from Egypt. On his return to Alexandria, he held a huge victory parade and delivered a speech denouncing his alliance with Octavian. He also declared that he was gifting various parts of the newly invaded land to his three children by Cleopatra, and that she was to be the queen of Egypt alongside her son by Caesar, Caesarion. The nail in the coffin came when he affirmed that Caesarion was the legitimate son and heir of Caesar. Of all of Antony's proclamations, this one had the effect of jeopardizing Octavian's position of power back in Rome.

Mark Antony was eventually stripped of his power by the Senate, who agreed that he had started wars without authority from Rome, had given away Roman land to his children, and that he was guilty of a number of other charges. In 32 BC, the Senate officially declared war on Cleopatra alone, a political nuance to appease some of Antony's loyal supporters and to distance Octavian from the fact that yet another civil war was starting.

It culminated in a huge clash at sea in 31 BC known as the Battle of Actium, in which Octavian was victorious. Antony had heard a rumour that Cleopatra was dead, and so he stabbed himself. Only then did he learn the rumour wasn't true, and he was carried to her before dying in her arms. Cleopatra later committed suicide before she could be brought as a prisoner to Rome to be executed. The victory created one sole ruler in Octavian, and he was given the title *imperator*, from where we get the word 'emperor', the first in Rome to bear this title. It heralded a shift from the power struggles, conspiracies and murders of the Roman Republic, and launched a new era: the Roman Empire.

Pax Romana

The term *Pax Romana* – 'Roman Peace' – refers to a period of 200 years that started with the ascension of Augustus Caesar as the first emperor of a new Roman Empire in 27 BC. There had been decades of political chaos, from Julius Caesar's civil war, his increasingly autocratic rule, and utterly disturbing assassination, followed by Augustus' own civil war to depose – and kill – Mark Antony.

If the transformation from Roman Republic to Roman Empire was to be successful, it was imperative that Augustus instilled a sense of calm and stability. At the same time, he knew that expansion of the Roman world through military campaigns was going to be needed to ensure a continued flow of wealth – and slaves – to the seat of power in Rome. Augustus' strategy with the Roman army was to secure their loyalty. He did this by moving the onus of the provision of soldiers' pensions from corrupt generals to the state itself, thereby reducing

---

The doubling in size of the Roman world that happened during Augustus' reign heralded the golden age of the civilization, with huge advancements in technology, architecture and culture. It really was the heyday of Rome, brought about by a leader who wanted to expand not just Rome, but Roman Peace, to the edges of the known world.

---

the risk of breakaway legions and military coups.

He focused his expansion in areas that would be most easily captured and defended, and allowed the annexed people to continue to practise their own religions and customs in most cases. As soon as you had been conquered, you were a part of the Roman Empire and therefore instantly at peace with it, whether you liked it or not. But by adopting and encouraging local customs and religion, Augustus' military progress to cover a quarter of the world's population was done with tact as well as force.

His deliberate policies made Augustus Caesar an incredibly popular emperor, who ruled until his death as an old man in AD 14.

CHAPTER 5

PHILOSOPHY

GREEK PHILOSOPHY

Thales

Thales was a philosopher, mathematician, engineer, astronomer and scientist born in Miletus on the modern-day Turkish coast in about 620 BC. As some thinkers started wanting to explain the world around them without resorting to mythology, Thales is known as the first to do so. It was nearly three hundred years later that the philosopher Aristotle claimed Thales as the first natural philosopher. That refers to his desire to understand the world and what it was made from. Thales theorized that there must be one origin matter from which everything was made, known as the *arche* – or 'the beginning'.

In seeking this origin matter, Thales supposed that all things must be able to be made from it, and must be able to return to it. He settled on water being that matter. He had observed water taking on its various forms as liquid, mist and ice, and saw how it was the nourishment for all forms of life and growth. Studying the silty flow of the river Meander drying up as it passed through Miletus, he also felt he had witnessed water slowly transforming into mud and earth. This is the original winding river, from where we get the word 'meander'.

Thales supposed that the whole world floated on water. If

everything is made from water, he reasoned, there would be a certain buoyancy of all physical things that would allow it to remain afloat. He explained that it was rough seas below the floating Earth that were the cause of earthquakes felt at surface level. Despite that, it is possible that Thales held that the Earth was spherical. Scholars – even those 2,000 years before Columbus' confirmation – debated a flat Earth versus a spherical one. Thales had a keen understanding of astronomy, even to the point where he was able to predict a solar eclipse, and set the solstices and equinoxes, and he was able to predict the location of constellations. Later interpretations of this knowledge point to the fact that he could not have come to any other conclusion than a round Earth.

It is said that he was so obsessed with observing the heavens that he wasn't paying attention to where he was walking and fell into a well.

Pythagoras

Pythagoras is known today for his theory on right-angled triangles, $a^2 + b^2 = c^2$, but he was so much more than that. He was also a philosopher, an astronomer, a priest in Egypt, the leader of a religious order in Italy, and a vegetarian. He lived on the Greek island of Samos in the sixth century BC, and would visit Thales and his student Anaximander, undoubtably being influenced by their teachings. Their interest in cosmology is said to have been influential in

Pythagoras' decision to spend much of his young adult life as a priest in Egypt to explore these disciplines further.

He eventually set up a philosophical school on Samos, and then in about 520 BC, he travelled to Croton in southern Italy and set up an institution that was part religious sect, part philosophy school. Followers of his teachings lived a strict life with no possessions and a plain vegetarian diet, and somewhat deified their leader. One local was so keen to join the school that he launched an attack on it when refused access in around 500 BC, which led to the deaths of many of its inhabitants. It is said that Pythagoras fled to Metapontium, where he died not long afterwards.

The mathematical theorem that bears Pythagoras' name was known before his time; the Babylonians were using it some one thousand years before him. However, it is Pythagoras or the followers in his philosophical schools who offered geometric proof of why the theorem is true. The Pythagoreans are also credited with the definitions and construction of regular geometric shapes and different types of triangle, and discovering irrational numbers. Pythagoras barely separated his philosophy from his number-crunching, and considered that everything in the universe could be broken down mathematically. He assigned personalities and attributes to different numbers, giving them gender and degrees of beauty.

Outside of the classroom, Pythagoras' influence has been extraordinary. The principle behind the theorem he proved has countless uses for our measurement of buildings, geology and the universe. His mathematical philosophy also stretched into music theory, devising principles around how to tune strings by their length and find perfect harmonies through mathematical ratios. He then even transposed this theory of harmony onto the spheres of the Earth and other planets to explain how the universe rotated around us in orbital resonance. His use of numbers and mathematical theory in philosophy and in the way he sought to understand the world also had a huge influence on the theory of numerology.

Heraclitus

Heraclitus was a philosopher of the late sixth century BC. He lived in the phenomenally preserved city of Ephesus on what is the modern-day Turkish coast. He was not far from the thinkers of Miletus and was not worried about contradicting his predecessors. His approach was as a metaphysical philosopher, looking for a universal law of physics that governed all things he observed in the world. He called this the *Logos* (the 'Word' or 'Truth'), to which all things belong or of which all things are a part.

His thinking can sometimes be quite difficult to grasp, sounding quite theoretical. Even ancient scholars found his ideas challenging, and Heraclitus' response was that most people were idiots who refused to understand the truth even after they had heard it. His key theories were of flux and unity. He described the physical world as being in a state of constant change and movement, using the metaphor of the river to explain what he meant: it is not possible to step into the same river twice. While the river retains its presence, the water is never the same from one moment to the next.

He sees the world in a tension of opposites. You need day to have night, winter to have summer, war to have peace, young to have old. This balance exists in all things, and both states exist at the same time; the youth and the old person exist in the same body. The importance of Heraclitus' thinking is that he takes the concepts of his predecessors and goes one step further. It is not just the physical world he is concerned with, but the metaphysical world. He is the first philosopher to bring human values into his discourse, something that changes scholarly investigations moving forwards.

Socrates

The influence of Socrates on the world of philosophy is so great that Greek philosophers that predate him are described as being Pre-Socratic. Such is the turning point that he represents in his field. As each scholar builds on the ideas of those that went before, you can see the complexity of their thinking evolve. They move from being concerned with what the world is made from, to thinking more about what it means to be part of Greek society. While Thales and his students debated whether water, air or earth were the origin matter of the universe, Socrates, who was

Socrates (c. 470–399 BC) had a profound influence on Western philosophy.

born in Athens around 470 BC, had discussions with the Athenian elite about the true meaning of virtue, of justice and of courage.

None of Socrates' thinking is written by the philosopher himself. Instead, almost all of his theories and studies are presented as dialogues written by his student Plato. He does also turn up as a character of ridicule in the comedy plays of Aristophanes, where he is portrayed as an eccentric atheist. The real mark of a Socratic dialogue is the skill with which he directs the conversation through the art of questioning alone. He challenges his sometimes exasperated companions on their thinking as they grapple with the definition of courage, for example. In the dialogues written by Plato, Socrates creates scenarios that systematically dismantle what his interlocutors initially hold to be true. Piece by piece, he pulls their argument apart until they are forced to reconsider what they understand of these complex definitions.

Rather than trying to put across any particular viewpoint, Socrates' skill is in helping his companions to really consider what they think. He famously quipped that the only thing he could be truly sure of was that he knew nothing at all. The discussions allow a glimpse into daily Athenian life, as they take place while Socrates is in situations such as leaving a theatre in the evening, and the dialogues are as challenging of our understanding now as they would have been to read 2,500 years ago.

Eventually, Socrates' notoriety as the atheist scholar would become his undoing. In 399 BC, he was put on trial for corrupting the minds of Athens' youth and for his atheism. He was found guilty and sentenced to death by drinking poisonous hemlock at the age of seventy-one.

Aristotle

Aristotle was a student of Plato for twenty years in the fourth century BC. Clearly influenced by Plato's keen study of Socrates' dialogues, Aristotle became most associated with logic, deductive reasoning and validating argument through rationality. He creates a new standard for definition and clarity in scientific language – and therefore in scientific thinking. An example of Aristotelian logic is the concept known as a syllogism, such as this: 'All men are mortal; Socrates is a man; therefore, Socrates is mortal.'

While all of that may sound utterly obvious to us a couple of millennia later, Aristotle's analysis of how we use language to describe our thinking was ground-breaking at the time. It was not just the language he was able to codify, but the thinking itself. He was the first person to put letters into his logic sentences (for example: 'All X are mortal; Y is an X; therefore, Y is mortal.'). It is a logic system that is still used in school algebra tests and scientific study alike today.

Like many of the philosophers of the ancient world, Aristotle was a polymath with wide-ranging contributions to the world of ethics, politics, mathematics and physics, and he was the first known zoologist. His desire for learning and logic guided him to be the first person to categorize the different scientific disciplines. He was the first to organize his school into a set syllabus and courses, and he was the first ever curator of a research library for himself and his students to benefit from.

The Schools of Philosophy

With so many competing scientific and philosophical ideologies, many of the notable philosophers of Ancient Greece created their own physical schools where they busied themselves with study, debate and defining their theories of the world and of society. The period after Aristotle, from about 323 BC up until the rise of the Roman Empire in the first century BC, is known as the Hellenistic period of philosophy and is centred on four main schools of thought: the Epicureans, the Cynics, the Stoics and the Skeptics.

The Epicureans are often mistakenly categorized as hedonists, and the word is used interchangeably with that idea today. Epicurus' school in a garden near Athens did ask its followers to seek out pleasure and avoid pain, but not purely as a pursuit of luxury and excess. In fact, his thinking asked students to find pleasure in simple things, and to accept that some pain was necessary if it led to pleasure later on. It sought out a humble and happy existence, rather than a hedonistic lifestyle.

The Cynics were a less structured movement in Hellenistic philosophical thinking. This free-thinking band of rebels shunned societal norms and instead aimed to achieve a life that was more in accordance with nature than the rigours of Athenian society. The name Cynics means 'The Dogs', either a disparaging name given to them by non-Cynics, or a rebellious name they chose for themselves. One notable Cynic was Diogenes of Sinope, who was known for urinating on people in retaliation for being called a Dog. The Cynics lived simply, almost as animals, because they maintained that we need very little to be happy.

The Stoics took some of the principles of Cynicism, but brought it back to the structure and polymathematic enquiry that the other schools of philosophy were known for. Zeno of Citium set up the Stoic school around 300 BC, where they studied logic, physics and ethics in a tradition that lasted several hundred years. Stoics believed it wiser to focus on the things we have control over – to control our impulses and desires; and not to worry about the things we have no control over – our possessions, status or death. Their ideal of giving no concern to things like death is often misinterpreted in a very unemotional way, and we use the word 'stoic' today to refer to the (traditionally British) 'stiff upper lip'. However, this is not the characteristic that comes across in the calm acceptance of ancient Stoicism.

The Skeptics arose around the same time as the Stoics. While the Stoics claimed to have a clear understanding of truth in nature and the universe, with their 'it is what it is' approach to the world, the Skeptics took the opposite stance: they questioned everything. The word *skeptic* means 'enquirer', and their founder Arcesilaus would eagerly argue both for and against a particular argument, until it became clear that no side could be trusted as the truth. This left the Skeptic to trust only one thing: the thing that they could observe and experience, and no more.

Roman Philosophy

Lucretius

Lucretius was a Roman poet and philosopher thought to have lived from 99 to 55 BC, known mainly for his poem *De Rerum Natura* (*On the Nature of Things*). He follows the Epicurean school of Greek philosophy, which advocates for finding pleasure and peace in a simple life, and avoiding pain unless it is necessary for later gain. The poem is written across six books, and gives a naturalistic explanation of the universe from its origin to its future.

Like many Romans, he is almost certain to have studied the original texts of the Ancient Greek philosophers that predate him by many centuries. Particularly, the Pre-Socratic philosophers engaged in this sort of discussion about what everything in the universe was actually made from. In an age before the equipment, laws and equations that modern scientists can take for granted, scientific study was left to philosophers to muse upon as theories rather than being based on evidential fact.

Lucretius gives a thorough exposition of Epicurean theories throughout his work, including the idea that everything in the universe is made from microscopic particles known as atoms. The word 'atom' comes from the Greek word meaning 'uncuttable', and refers to the final point at which all matter can no longer be divisible. Contrary to modern understanding, Epicureans also believed that the soul itself was made of these atoms, which gives some insight into how physically real they imagined the afterlife, the Underworld and perhaps the rest of ancient mythology to be. Despite that, Lucretius distanced his philosophy from the gods that so many dedicated their lives to. He believed the pantheon of gods to be real, but rejected the idea that the gods had direct input into the daily lives of humans. Epicureanism teaches its followers to be delighted with the life they can create, rather than be hopeful to the gods for more, or fearful of their retribution.

The way in which Greek Pre-Socratic philosophers and Roman Epicureans like Lucretius delve into the physical make-up of the universe helps them make sense of the world around them. There is a certain grounding effect in understanding the natural world, especially in an age when everything unknown was explained away by myth. *De Rerum Natura* is extraordinary in how it straddles poetry, philosophy and scientific enquiry, and it remained an important influence on each of those fields for many centuries.

Seneca

Born in modern-day Córdoba in Spain in 4 BC, Seneca was part of a well-connected and wealthy family. Few others could afford themselves a life of study, debate and philosophizing. He travelled to Rome as a young boy to study in one of the philosophical schools, which used Roman interpretations of the Stoic and Pythagorean ideals. His intellect would see him enter the world of law and politics, where he was part of the inner circle of the emperors of Rome. Emperor Caligula wanted to kill him, while Claudius banished him temporarily to Corsica, and he wrote Nero's first public speech in office.

During Seneca's exile and attempted retirement, he wrote many letters and treatises that are considered important artefacts in the Stoic movement, covering topics including happiness, wisdom, grief, morality and the brevity of life – alongside his thoughts on the dangers of public baths and large crowds. The Stoic perspective is one of a level-headed and rational life, not marred by extreme emotion – a depiction that is at odds with the wealth, power and scandal that we know were features of Seneca's life off the pages.

In his 124 *Moral Letters to Lucilius*, we see an old man write frequently about the fleeting nature of time to the governor of Sicily. Many letters start by observing some part of daily Roman life, which Seneca uses as a springboard for his philosophical ideas and advice.

He got perhaps too close to the tyrannical and chaotic Nero, first being implicated alongside Nero in the murder of the emperor's mother, and finally accused of plotting to kill Nero himself. That accusation led to him losing his life.

Marcus Aurelius

Another notable political philosopher was the emperor Marcus Aurelius. He spent much of his reign on military campaigns around central Europe, where he found the time during the AD 170s to write down his ideas on Stoicism in a collection known as *The Meditations*. They seem to be the notebooks of a keen student of philosophy, written for himself as an exercise in working through some philosophical theories, so that he may himself come to understand them better. He wrote them in Ancient Greek, a language that all well-educated people in Rome studied, and that perhaps gave them a closer connection to the original Stoics that he was influenced by.

His Greek notes were originally titled *τὰ εἰς ἑαυτόν* ('*ta eis eauton*') – 'Things to oneself' – so it's possible that they were something like personal diary entries that helped clarify his own resolve before going into battle. He very likely did not intend for them to be published. The fact that these are the extremely intimate ponderings of the world's most powerful person at that time make *The Meditations* fascinating on a historical and even human perspective, as well as from a philosophical viewpoint.

Stoicism is anchored in a level-headed acceptance of the things we cannot control, rather than the common misinterpretation in the present day of a 'stoic' attitude being cold and unfeeling. Marcus Aurelius emphasizes that any stress we experience is not caused by external events, but rather by our own interpretation of those events. He argues that we have the ability to change our perspective on a situation we have no control over, to alter its impact on us.

The Meditations teaches its readers to ground themselves in core virtues such as courage, wisdom and justice when facing adversity. These are the sorts of concepts that the earlier Greek philosopher Socrates sought to define, using his dialogue and interrogation technique to challenge his companions – and the readers of those dialogues – on what they really meant when they used words like 'justice'. Socrates was a significant influence on the Stoic school of philosophy, and Marcus Aurelius would have been very familiar with the work attributed to him. If you have truly explored what it means to have courage, to act with justice and to conduct yourself with wisdom, you can avoid emotional reactions to the obstacles you face, and meet them instead with level-headed responses that accord with the core virtues of Stoicism.

Delving into the mind of a political and military leader at his most vulnerable moments during war gives us a real test of Stoicism as a school of philosophy. If it can give strength to Marcus Aurelius in those situations, then surely there are lessons to draw from it for everyday obstacles.

CHAPTER 6

LITERATURE

Epic Poetry

Homer

Some of the oldest legends ever told are attributed to the poet Homer. He is said to have lived in the eighth century BC on what is now the Turkish coast, and his name appears as the author of two epic poems of the classical world: the *Iliad* and the *Odyssey*. These poems have given us so much of what we understand about Greek mythology: the Cyclops, the Trojan Horse, journeys into the Underworld, and disputes between the gods.

Even in the days of the Ancient Greeks, Homer's work was ancient stuff. Those two gigantic works, and all of the imaginative mythology they contain, were committed to writing around the same time as Greece's writing system was invented. They were studied in the schools of Greece and Rome for hundreds of years after they first appeared, and were just as important then as they are now in helping to form a picture of what the Ancient Greek civilization was all about.

What's extraordinary about the epic poems is that they are written in a strange form of Greek only found in a handful of very ancient texts, which has become known as Homeric Greek. The verses mix up different Greek dialects, sometimes within the same sentence, and even use word forms from different eras of Greek linguistic history. It's like reading a poem that contains Shakespearean English, modern phrases, Chaucerian vocabulary and Scottish slang all in the same sentence.

It becomes clear that the poems could not have been written down by one man at all. Instead, the 30,000 lines of poetry contained in the *Iliad* and the *Odyssey* were passed on orally by wandering bards, who would entertain crowds with their fantastical legends as they travelled. Impossible as that may sound, the rhythmic music of the poetry and the many repeated phrases and verses would have allowed the bards to weave their version of the tale on any given evening. And each subsequent generation of bards and storytellers added local dialects and up-to-date vernacular as they passed on the thrilling myths of war, love, monsters and gods, long before they were put down into writing.

So, even if Homer the poet didn't really exist in the way we might imagine, the poems and legends attributed to him are among the oldest stories in existence. It is remarkable that the tales of the Trojan War, of Odysseus and of the Cyclops helped the Ancient Greeks to define their own identity and mythological history, in the same way that we continue to build a picture of their civilization through those tales today.

The Iliad

Homer's *Iliad* is set in the final years of the ten-year Trojan War, in which Greek armies are besieging the ancient city of Troy, and the action largely takes place on the plains outside the city walls. The poem's title refers to one of the names given to that city, Ilium. In much of classical literature, the fortunes and misfortunes that mortals experience on Earth are as a result of the disputes, jealousy, hinderance or encouragement of the gods on Mount Olympus, and the twenty-four books that make up the *Iliad* are no exception.

The problems begin when Zeus, king of the gods, gives an apple to one of the world's most eligible bachelors and prince of Troy, Paris. Tasked with presenting the apple to the goddess that he finds most beautiful, Paris is put in an unenviable position of choosing between the goddess of love, Aphrodite, the queen of the gods, Hera, and the goddess of wisdom, Athena. His apple goes to Aphrodite, who rewards him by making the most beautiful woman in the world fall in love with him. The only problem is that this woman, Helen, is already married to a Greek king, Menelaus, who doesn't take kindly to his wife being stolen away to Troy. This is how the Trojan War begins.

Among the alliance of Greek armies are military leader Achilles, his young companion and possible lover Patroclus, King Agamemnon of Mycenae and his brother, the cuckolded King Menclaus of Sparta. Fighting for the other side and defending the city of Troy is military leader

Hector, alongside his brother, Paris, and their father, King Priam of Troy. Nearly half of Book 2 of the *Iliad* is taken up by the lengthy listing of all the different contingents of both the Greek and Trojan armies as they prepare for battle. While not a fascinating read, it gives a sense of scale to the two entire nations about to clash, and makes the later battle scenes and loss of life much more personal. For those who originally listened to the poem across the different areas of Greece, it would have been an effective way to excite them as their region got a call-out in Homer's work. It's possible that, in the oral tradition of the travelling bards, the list of regions and characters became longer and longer as it travelled around Greece from one town to another.

In Book 16 of the poem, Achilles' young companion Patroclus naively decides to join the battlefield wearing Achilles' armour. In a case of mistaken identity, he is killed by Hector, and this news sends Achilles into such a rage that he goes on a gory and violent rampage, with a power and ferocity spurred on by his grief. The two opposing leaders eventually come face-to-face on the plains outside Troy, and Hector is killed. Achilles is still so consumed by grief that he spends twelve whole days brutally mistreating the dead body – most notably by threading a chord through Hector's heel tendons, tying him to a chariot and dragging him at speed across the plains. Anything other than a proper ceremony and burial is seen as truly barbaric in the eyes of the Greeks. Achilles eventually sees sense and returns the body to the Trojans and allows King Priam enough time to give his son an appropriate ceremony. This is where the *Iliad* ends.

The Odyssey

The far-reaching consequences of the Trojan War are picked up in this second epic poem attributed to Homer. In the twenty-four books that make up the *Odyssey*, we follow the story of the Greek military leader and king of Ithaca, Odysseus. With his fleet of twelve ships, Odysseus makes the long journey home from the war across the Mediterranean, adding another ten years to his ordeal as he is constantly blown off course and interrupted in his quest.

Back home in Ithaca, his wife Penelope must wait twenty years for her king to return, forced to stave off an increasingly impatient group of 108 suitors who are after the throne. For three of those years, she is able to delay any remarriage by claiming that she will choose her new husband just as soon as she has finished weaving a funeral shroud for her father-in-law. However, each night she unpicks that day's weaving to buy herself more time to await Odysseus' return.

The hero's journey is a hazardous and thrilling adventure, as he encounters a series of monsters, gods and lovers along the way. At times, the progress of Odysseus and his men is aided by the intervention of his guiding goddess Athena, and at other times, it is delayed and obstructed by the intervention of Poseidon and other less sympathetic gods.

For seven years, the nymph Calypso enchants Odysseus with song and lust and keeps him captive on her faraway island. On another island, his men meet the lotus-eaters, whose delicious lotus fruit causes them to utterly forget about their homecoming, until they are dragged away from their stupor. Elsewhere, Odysseus gets trapped in the cave of the giant, one-eyed Cyclops, and must use his cunning to find his way out. On another island, the goddess Circe turns half of Odysseus' men into pigs before seducing him into staying put for a year.

Finally leaving Circe's island, Odysseus' fleet must sail past the Sirens. These two creatures sit high on a rocky island, and their magical, piercing song will transfix anyone who hears it. Odysseus' men all block their ears with beeswax, but the hero wants to hear this unearthly sound. He is tied fast to the mast as they row by the dangerous

Odysseus and the Sirens are depicted on this red-figure vase, c. 480–470 BC.

rocks. As the captivating song reaches Odysseus' ears, enticing him to sail ever closer to them and to the craggy coast, he begs his men to untie him and begs them to slow the boats, but the beeswax saves them all from the temptation of certain destruction. That is where we get the modern word 'siren' from.

In the end, Odysseus is the only one of his 600 crew members to make it home. After first disguising himself as an old man to test Penelope's fidelity, he murders all the suitors in utterly gory scenes, and reclaims his rightful place on the throne of Ithaca.

Virgil

Born in 70 BC, Virgil is Rome's most famous poet. But to understand his role in Roman history, we must first look at what was going on politically at the time.

Augustus Caesar came to power as the first emperor of Rome in 27 BC, following decades of political unrest, civil war and the assassination of his great-uncle Julius Caesar. His route to power was not an easy one, and he needed to unite the sprawling population if he was going to rule successfully. He transformed the Roman Republic into the Roman Empire, and went about expanding its borders considerably, with landgrabs in modern-day Spain, Portugal, Switzerland, Germany, Austria, Slovenia, Hungary, Israel, Tunisia, Libya and beyond.

The Romans never hid their adoration of Ancient Greek

culture, literature and power, much of which would have felt ancient even to your average Roman. So, when the time came for Augustus to find a way to bring all those newly annexed people into the Roman fold, he first looked to the epic poems created by the Greeks. What better way to show the whole Mediterranean what it meant to be a Roman than by creating a new origin story in the form of an epic poem? Homer's Greek works would have been widely studied and retold in Rome, so recreating a Roman version of those familiar tales would at the same time feel ancient and weighty, yet allow Augustus to create his own definition of what it meant to be Roman.

This is where Virgil comes in. Already a well-respected poet, Virgil was commissioned to write the *Aeneid*: Rome's new origin story, which borrowed heavily the themes and mythologies of Homer's Ancient Greek legends, but with a distinctly Augustan flavour.

The Aeneid

Virgil's *Aeneid* is Rome's very own epic poem, retelling the origin story of the Roman Empire for an ever-expanding audience of existing and newly annexed Roman citizens. Split over twelve books and nearly ten thousand lines of poetry, it starts as all good epic poems do in the classical world: at the Trojan War. That is the same war that Homer's *Iliad* describes, and the same war from which Homer's hero Odysseus must make his long journey home. However,

Virgil's twist on the customs established by Homer is that he focuses on a hero from the Trojan side rather than the Greek side.

The story follows the Trojan hero Aeneas as he journeys away from the fallen city of Troy after the great war, in order to found the new civilization of Rome. Broadly speaking, the first six books of Virgil's *Aeneid* share similarities with the hero's journey seen in Homer's *Odyssey*, with faraway lands and fantastical creatures, and the second six books share more similarities with the warmongering of the *Iliad*, with Aeneas battling the local Italians on whose land Rome must be built.

Aeneas is a Trojan hero related to Troy's king, descended from Troy's founding father, and was the son of the goddess of love herself, Venus. What better lineage could there be to found the city of Rome? So as not to entirely do away with Rome's other very famous origin story – that of Romulus, Remus and the wolf – Virgil goes on to describe Aeneas as an ancestor of those boys, who in turn are ancestors of the poem's sponsor, Augustus Caesar. The political aim of this work of literature is not at all subtle.

As the paradigm for the model citizen of the Roman Empire, Aeneas must go through many hardships but always puts Rome first before all other personal desires. His journey home sees Aeneas and what remains of the Trojan people settle in the city of Carthage. There, he enraptures Queen Dido with his stories of adventure, bravery and loss. The pair soon fall in love, and during a particularly heavy rainstorm devised by the gods, find themselves sheltering

Dido building Carthage, J. M. W. Turner's 1815 oil painting of the legendary queen founding her city.

in a cave together, where the union is sealed, if not quite formalized.

As time goes by, the Trojan refugees grow restless, and the Carthaginian people become less hospitable to their lingering guests. The gods argue and negotiate between themselves as to whether the hero stays in Carthage or continues his journey to found Rome. But ultimately it is Jupiter, king of the gods, who makes his opinion unequivocal: the hero must meet his destiny.

Heartbroken, but resolute in his mission, Aeneas instructs his people to ready the ships. Dido soon hears about his plan to desert her, and flies through Carthage in a rage until she finds him. Aeneas wants nothing more than to stay with her, but he has the warning from Jupiter ringing in his ears. He suppresses his abject sorrow and knows he must cause utter heartbreak to his beloved queen.

As the hero's ships are prepared, Dido has all of Aeneas' possessions piled high in the palace courtyard: their marital bed, his robes, images of him and his hunting dagger all lie on top of a huge pyre ready to burn. At first light, the ships set sail. Dido's rage and passion drive her through the palace. She climbs the towering pyre and, just as her maids enter the courtyard, she falls on Aeneas' dagger and collapses onto their marital bed. The fire is lit, and out to sea, Aeneas turns back to Carthage one last time. He sees the soaring flames that now light his way as he continues on to Rome.

GREEK TRAGEDY

Theatre was at the heart of Ancient Greek culture. The ruins of spectacular theatres can be seen across the Greek world, with their instantly recognizable semicircular bowl construction. The size of these ruins offers a glimpse into the popularity of this pastime, with the Theatre of Dionysus, carved into the side of the Acropolis in Athens, said to have seated 17,000 audience members if not more. The Great Theatre of Ephesus on Turkey's coast held a similar crowd, and still to this day offers the most breathtaking sunset views over the Mediterranean as the world's orchestras and actors perform beneath you nearly 2,300 years after its first construction.

This is the setting in which Greek tragedies were performed. They are a style of play that combines fast-paced dialogue with choral interludes and often depicts the heartbreaking downfall of a hero. The plays are typically anchored in a terrible prophecy made about the protagonist. In seeking to avoid the dreadful prediction, the characters set about actions that in fact cause it to come true. There are no happy endings in this genre as the audience is made to see that we cannot outrun our destiny, regardless of how cleverly we try to avoid it.

Some Greek tragic playwrights mastered the art of the trilogy well before Hollywood or Bollywood, with three parts continuing the story from one unfortunate generation to another. Theatres would often show all three plays on the same day, making it quite the morose day out for Greek society. Elsewhere, festivals to Dionysus would task different playwrights with writing their version of the same story for the ultimate pop culture competitions, which is how we have ended up with the same titles written by multiple authors.

So, as you read about some of the most loved stories in Greek tragedy, imagine the back-and-forth dialogue as the heroes face up to their gut-wrenching downfall, hear the haunting song of the choir echoing around the towering rows of seats, visualize the spectacular natural backdrop as 17,000 people fall silent in sorrow, and be entertained by the competing playwrights fighting for audience attention and adoration.

> The most influential trio of tragedy writers are Aeschylus, Sophocles and Euripides, all of whom battled for popularity in the fifth century BC.

Agamemnon

Often considered the father of Greek tragedy, playwright Aeschylus presented his performance of *Agamemnon* as part of a trilogy known as the *Oresteia*. With these plays, Aeschylus won the coveted first prize in the competition of Athens' prestigious Dionysia festival in 458 BC and cemented the archetype for the Greek tragedy. The trilogy is named after Orestes, the son of Agamemnon, whose cursed family is beset with misfortune across the generations.

Agamemnon is the king of Mycenae and one of the key Greek leaders who besieged Troy and ultimately conquered the city in the ten-year war that inspired so much of classical literature. Aeschylus' play tells of the king's ill-fated return to Mycenae following the war. In the decade that has passed, his wife, Clytemnestra, has fallen in love with Aegisthus, and the two lovers have been plotting the murder of King Agamemnon whenever he may return from the war.

Clytemnestra has never forgiven her husband for killing their daughter Iphigenia. On the way to Troy at the start of the war, Agamemnon had angered the goddess Artemis as the fleet was gathering in Aulis. The spiteful goddess wouldn't give the Greeks the favourable winds they needed to reach Troy unless Agamemnon lured Iphigenia to Aulis and sacrificed her in Artemis' name. Clytemnestra's lover Aegisthus also carries his own motives for wanting the king dead, from generations of the two families fighting over the seat of Mycenae.

Agamemnon returns to Mycenae with his concubine Cassandra, taken from the Trojans after the war. The young girl is predestined to utter true prophecies, but which no one will believe, and she does so with the murder of both Agamemnon and herself. Clytemnestra lays down a red carpet of robes for Agamemnon to walk upon through the large, stone gates of the palace. This darkly insincere welcome forces Agamemnon to knowingly anger the gods with an excessive display of regal arrogance.

Keeping up the act of a dutiful wife, she lures him inside, runs him a bath, then ties him up with a net before brutally stabbing him three times – the final stab as he lies on the floor spluttering blood. The queen, who is much reviled in classical literature, rules over Mycenae with Aegisthus at her side.

Today, you can still walk through the ruins of the huge palace where Agamemnon's cruel murder is supposed to have taken place, walking through the towering gates through which he was welcomed by his murderous wife.

Electra

Aeschylus continues his trilogy, the *Oresteia*, with this play named after the daughter of Clytemnestra and Agamemnon. His contemporary playwrights Sophocles and Euripides also penned versions of her story. Clytemnestra is ruling in Mycenae with her new husband, Aegisthus, but is wary of her children, Orestes and Electra. Both have been sent away – partly to protect them from Aegisthus' violence and partly to protect Clytemnestra from her children's retaliation.

Orestes is safeguarded in his banishment and raised by the king of Phocis, while Electra is married off to a benevolent farmer. As an adult, Orestes arrives at Electra's home with his friend Pylades, and initially does not reveal his identity. Electra tells him the terrible story of her father's murder at her mother's hand, and how she longs to be reunited with her brother. When Orestes' true identity is made clear, the two siblings forge a plan.

Clytemnestra is invited to Electra's humble farm under the pretext that her daughter has given birth. Meanwhile, Orestes and Pylades make their way to murder Aegisthus. As Aegisthus performs a divine sacrifice to the gods, Orestes savagely stabs him before revealing his true identity. When he arrives at Electra's home, Orestes begins to doubt whether he can go through with killing his own mother. Has this tragic family not suffered enough death? It is Electra who guides her brother through his reluctance, speaking of a prophecy that foretold he would murder his mother.

With the guiding hand of Electra on the sword, Orestes drives his blade down into Clytemnestra's throat. Both siblings are beside themselves with guilt, but are pacified by the gods that what passed was the just outcome for Clytemnestra's terrible crime.

Oedipus

The tragic tale of Oedipus is told by several Greek poets and authors, but most movingly by Sophocles in his play *Oedipus Rex*. The play follows another cursed family, the house of Thebes, and it is a grim unravelling of the title character's life and the gradual destruction of everything he knows. To watch the play performed or even to read it can leave you with an emptiness and heartache that is as real now as it would have been to an audience in 429 BC. Human grief has not altered in 2,500 years.

Oedipus is the king of Thebes, and rules with his beloved queen, Jocasta. The gods have beset the city with a plague, due to the unresolved murder of Thebes' previous king, and Jocasta's former husband, Laius. Oedipus seeks help from the blind prophet Tiresias to identify the murderer of the old king and bring justice and harmony back to the city. Tiresias at first refuses to divulge the unspeakable truth that he foresees, but is eventually forced to utter the words that will bring so much pain: Oedipus himself is the murderer that he seeks.

Oedipus is outraged by the blind prophet's nonsense – of course he isn't the murderer! His wife Jocasta tries to appease her husband by sharing her own story of how inaccurate these oracles can be. Many years ago, she too had been told a terrible prophecy that her own son would kill his father and marry his mother. Clearly that was nonsense, since the old king, Laius, was killed by bandits at a crossroads on the way to Delphi and not by his own son. Oedipus pauses with a terrible sense of foreboding at the mention of Laius' murder; it sounds chillingly familiar.

A shepherd brings news to Thebes of the death of Oedipus' father in Corinth, which instantly delights the king. Surely this means he couldn't be the son that was prophesied to kill his own father. But further questioning reveals the horrendous truth: the king and queen of Corinth were not, in fact, Oedipus' real parents. When Laius and Jocasta had heard the original prediction that their son would kill one and marry the other, Laius ordered that the boy be killed. But Jocasta couldn't bear to kill her child, and so he was sent away and adopted by the king and queen of Corinth.

As their reality unravels, both Oedipus and Jocasta begin to grasp the dark truth of their marriage. Oedipus did indeed kill Laius – his true father – at that crossroads on the way to Delphi following a disagreement, neither man knowing who the other was. And just as the prophecy foretold, Oedipus came to Thebes and married his own mother. Their tragic fate is finally revealed, and Jocasta runs to her bedroom and hangs herself in utter grief at the terrible destiny they have all stumbled into. Oedipus crashes through the palace in despair, and when he finds his mother and wife hanging in the bedroom, takes two gold pins from her dress and digs them into his eyes, so that he may never see such horror again.

Antigone

One of the features that makes Greek tragedy so heartbreaking is how grief and misfortune follow a family from one generation on to the next. Sophocles continues the tragic history of the house of Thebes in the follow-up play about Oedipus' daughter, Antigone. In the aftermath of Oedipus and Jocasta's deaths, the sons of this incestuous marriage fought over who would take the throne. Both were killed in the ensuing war, and Jocasta's brother Creon willingly took his place as king of Thebes. In their death, Antigone's two brothers were not offered the same respect. One brother, Eteocles, was given a burial befitting a prince, whereas the other brother, Polyneices, was left to rot outside the city walls.

In Ancient Greek culture, such mistreatment of the dead was unspeakable. Without the proper rituals and a respectful burial, Polyneices' spirit would never find its way into the Underworld. Antigone steals out of the city and starts to bury her own brother, when she is captured and brought before Creon. She pleads with the new king to give Polyneices the rightful burial that every person deserves. Creon is outraged by her audacity and imprisons her in a cave with just enough food to keep her alive for a while, but where she will slowly wither away.

Antigone's fiancé, Haemon, is the son of the new king, but even he can't change Creon's mind about the terrible punishment she has to endure. The king likewise ignores the warning from Tiresias – the blind prophet whom Oedipus similarly dismissed in the previous play – that his actions will anger the gods. Meanwhile, the stench of Polyneices' corpse is overwhelming the city just as it is the fate of the play's tragic characters.

Haemon tries to free Antigone from her cave, but finds that she has hanged herself just as her mother Jocasta did in *Oedipus Rex*. Haemon kills himself in abject grief at the loss of his beloved fiancée, and this news in turn leads Haemon's mother, Eurydice, to kill herself too. King Creon, who has fought so hard to finally rule over Thebes, is left with the bodies of his wife and son, two tragic deaths caused only by his own actions.

COMEDY

Lysistrata

O ne of Ancient Greece's most prolific and outrageous comic playwrights was Aristophanes, and perhaps none of his plays is quite as salacious as *Lysistrata*. First performed in 411 BC, it tells of the Athenian woman Lysistrata, who is horrified by the ongoing Peloponnesian War. Gathering women from all the various city states involved in the war over control of Greek land, Lysistrata realizes that the men of Athens and Sparta will not listen to reason, and that there is only one thing that the women can control: sex. She convinces the women that they will all aggressively seduce their husbands, and then withhold sex until they force the men to abandon the war.

Despite being over 2,400 years old, the play offers a remarkably frank exploration of sex and gender, with these bold heroines at the heart of the action, even if they would have been originally played by men. As for the male characters, their increasingly unsatisfied libidos were visualized on stage by increasingly large comedy phalluses held between their legs. Visually and thematically, this really is quite the bawdy play, and gives an insight into a sense of humour that wouldn't be out of place in the British *Carry On* movies of the 1950s to 1970s.

The first act of defiance occurs when the old women of Athens take control of the Acropolis in the centre of the city, home to a brand-new building called the Parthenon. Used as the treasury, it is a strategically important site needed to continue with any warfare. A chorus of men arrive with torches, ready to set fire to the gates if the women don't relent. But the unstoppable women outsmart the men by pouring cold water on their flames and on their comically large penises.

As time goes by, both the men and Lysistrata's army of women wane in their resolve. One man approaches the Acropolis, weighed down by his absurd prosthetic. It is Kinesias in search of his wife, Myrrhine. Under Lysistrata's instructions, Myrrhine strings her husband along in a painfully slow seduction, first pulling out the bed, then going offstage to get a pillow, then again for a blanket, then for some oils. The audience would have been shrieking in laughter as Myrrhine finally turns away and locks herself on the Acropolis again, leaving Kinesias alone and visibly unsatisfied.

Finally, both the Spartan and Athenian men have had enough. They are desperate to resolve their sexual desire and send delegates to negotiate peace. Lysistrata brings out a beautiful, naked young woman called Reconciliation. Of course, the men can't take their eyes off her, and in their sexual stupor, they divide up her body in crude and detailed language as they discuss which bits of Greece will be divided between the two sides. War is ended, as is the sex strike, and all the men, women, Athenians and Spartans head to the Acropolis for what must have been one hell of a party.

The Oldest Joke Book
in the World

In the fourth century AD, two Greek men, Hierocles and Philagrios, set about compiling 265 of their favourite one-liners, a collection that has become the oldest joke book in existence. Originally titled *Philogelos* (often translated as *The Laughter-Lover*, although *The Joker* probably makes more sense), it gives an extraordinary insight into the everyday sense of humour of your average Roman, outside of the more considered scripts of comic plays or witty lines of poetry. (Rome had conquered Greece by this point, so the Greek men – and their Greek jokes – are officially Roman.)

So, what one-liners did these Greek Romans tell each other? The collection is divided into different categories: one set of jokes mocks an unknown idiot; another set mocks the smartarse; some jokes poke fun at the hapless apprentice; and others use regional citizens of the Roman Empire as the butt of the joke.

Some of the gags could feature in a stand-up act of one-liners today, whereas others don't stand the test of time or translation. Ancient Greek is quite a literal language, so simply stating that one thing is another thing sounded quite absurd to them – and therefore was utterly hilarious. Even if some lines don't work for our modern and translated ear, what remains clear is that flatulence has been funny for at least 1,600 years. Here's a selection of some of the oldest jokes humanity has on record:

A sick husband is on his last legs.
His wife says to him, 'If anything happens to you, I'll hang myself.'
He looks up at her and replies: 'Do it while I'm still alive, darling.'

Hairdresser: 'How shall I cut your hair?'
Client: 'In silence.'

Friend: 'Can I borrow a cloak – just to go down to the countryside?'
The Idiot: 'I've only got one that goes down to the ankle.'

Did you hear about the Abderite who was told that onions and cabbage cause wind? He took a sack of the vegetables out sailing with him on a calm day, and hung them from the stern.

LOVE POETRY

Pyramus and Thisbe

In AD 8, Roman poet Ovid penned *Metamorphoses*, a compendium of beautiful poetry that spans 12,000 lines across fifteen books and is one of the most important sources of classical mythology in existence. It catalogues the mythological history of the world, from the creation of the universe all the way up to the death and deification of Julius Caesar in 44 BC, combining Greek legends with Roman interpretation. As the name suggests, the stories are all about change and transformation. The protagonists of his tales often meet a grisly end, and are transformed into a well-known constellation, plant, animal or natural landmark. These are Ovid's own origin stories for the natural world around us.

In the story of Pyramus and Thisbe, there are more than a few similarities with Shakespeare's *Romeo and Juliet*. Shakespeare doesn't hide his adoration of Ovid's works, lifting an entire passage for a speech in *The Tempest* and even having a miniature play of Pyramus and Thisbe performed within *A Midsummer Night's Dream*.

In the walled city of Assyria live two families side by side. Pyramus is the handsome young son of one family, and Thisbe is the daughter of the other family, who is known across Babylonia for her beauty. The two have known each other since they could walk, and their love has grown as they have. But their fathers won't allow the pair to marry, and so the would-be lovers have to make do with the occasional glance and private smile.

However, love always finds a way. Between their homes is an unnoticed crack in the thick walls, and through this tiny gap the two are able to share whispers, blow kisses and feed their yearning. Each night they sit, together but alone, and sigh their vain hopes before a final goodnight. Eventually, they resolve that something has to change; if they are ever to be together, they must escape their parents and go beyond the city walls.

One night, Thisbe covers her face in a veil and slips out into the moonlight, unnoticed by her sleeping parents. Outside the city, she reaches the lovers' agreed meeting spot beneath a tall mulberry tree, overladen with white berries. As she catches her breath and laughs at what bravery love has given her, she detects something large moving through the bushes. It is the unmistakable shape of a fully grown lioness, jaws frothing red from a recent kill, making her way to drink from the stream. In a panic, Thisbe makes a dash for the shelter of a cave just behind her, dropping her veil in her haste.

When the lioness has quenched her thirst, she wanders back past the mulberry tree. She sniffs curiously at the veil on the ground, then claws at it and tears it with her bloody teeth before making her way back into the shadows. Just a moment later, Pyramus arrives, full of love and excitement.

But then he freezes. He spots Thisbe's veil, torn and bloody on the ground, and next to it the unmistakable paw prints of an adult lion.

He grabs the veil and kisses it desperately, mixing his tears with the blood. Desolate with grief and with the guilt that he should have come out ahead of poor Thisbe, Pyramus takes out his sword and slides it into his abdomen. Blood gushes out as he falls to the floor, soaking the ground so much that the white berries of the mulberry tree turn deep red. Now Thisbe returns, eager to tell her lover of her brave escape from the lioness. But she instantly sees the red berries on the tree and Pyramus lying at its roots. Crying into the night, she takes Pyramus' sword. His eyes open one last time to see Thisbe fall down onto the blade, still warm with his blood, and the lovers are dead. In the memory of this tragic tale, the berries of the mulberry tree still darken red as they ripen.

Orpheus and Eurydice

Another love story from Ovid's *Metamorphoses* tells of one of the rarest experiences in classical mythology: a journey into the Underworld. Only a handful of characters make it into the land of the dead and return, and Orpheus is one of the unhappy few.

On their wedding day, Orpheus and Eurydice could not be more in love. But when Hymen, the god of marriage, appears his ceremonial torch fails to light and casts a thick

Orpheus and Eurydice depicted in a mosaic panel at the Palais Garnier opera house, Paris.

black smoke into the lovers' eyes. This bad omen indeed plays out, as shortly afterwards, Eurydice is bitten on the ankle by a snake and is instantly dragged down into the Underworld. Orpheus' grief is unparalleled, and he expresses it the only way he knows how: by playing the lyre that was gifted to him by the god Apollo himself. The lamentation of this unearthly music stops the natural world in its tracks. His songs of grief even reach into the Underworld, whose eternal inhabitants are all struck silent by his sorrow.

Orpheus makes the unenviable journey down into the Underworld and pleads with its king and queen, Pluto and Persephone, to allow him more time with his new wife. Moved by his words, they agree to his request on one condition: that he must leave the land of the dead without once looking back at his wife until they reach the mortal world.

Everything goes to plan until the very last moments. Orpheus is at the very threshold of the Underworld and he can hear Eurydice behind him, still struggling on the difficult climb with her wounded ankle. He wants to make sure that she doesn't stumble, so looks briefly back. In an instant, his beloved wife falls back down into the shadowy depths with heartbreak in her eyes as she whispers: 'Goodbye.' Orpheus reaches out, but catches nothing but cold air. His wife has died for a second time.

Orpheus mourns by the Underworld's river Styx, pleading to revisit the rulers of death, but is denied. Eventually, he returns to the world of the living, where he spends three years in solitude. His chastity draws anger from local girls, who start to attack the singing widower. At first, his divine music shields him from their onslaught, but as their assault intensifies, even Apollo's lyre cannot protect him. Orpheus is brutally murdered and his body floats down the river.

Finally back in the Underworld, Orpheus relentlessly searches for Eurydice until they are reunited. Now as they walk, he can occasionally look back at his cherished wife, safe in the knowledge that they will be together for eternity.

CHAPTER 7

ART AND
ARCHITECTURE

GREEK ART AND ARCHITECTURE

The Parthenon

In the centre of the sprawling city of Athens lies the Acropolis, a towering flat-topped rock that dominates the skyline wherever you are looking from in the city. As a natural defence vantage point, the Acropolis came to house some of the most important sites of the Ancient Greek world, including the shimmering white Parthenon. Built in 438 BC, the Parthenon was a temple to the city's patron goddess, Athena, and also housed the city's treasury.

With its large rectangular shape and two layers of columns supporting a large gable roof, you might be excused for thinking the architectural design of the Parthenon is relatively simple. It is anything but. In fact, its remarkable design – elegant, welcoming and yet authoritative – barely uses a single straight line in its construction. Its architects, Ictinus and Callicrates, knew that long, straight lines in buildings of this size cause optical illusions that would make it look top-heavy, and that would make the columns look thinner in the middle as an observer looked up.

They countered this with optical illusions of their own. The whole foundation of the temple is curved both upwards and inwards in a very subtle dome – so the middle of the base is both slimmer and higher than at the corners. This also helps with draining rain water and any sacrificial blood that might need draining. The columns around the perimeter are curved inwards at an imperceptible incline that would see them meet in the middle over 2 kilometres (about 1.25 miles) above the Parthenon roof, and each column bulges in the middle and tapers at the top to draw the eyes gradually up to the heavens.

Although our image of ancient buildings and statues is of blinding white marble, the friezes of the Parthenon were originally painted in vivid blues, reds and greens.

In 1800, the British diplomat Lord Elgin stole these friezes and took them to the UK, where they still sit in the British Museum despite a decidedly undiplomatic standoff between the British and Greek governments. It wasn't until the 1930s that some overzealous museum restorers spotted unsightly remnants of paint on the statues, and gave them a thorough clean to return them to the white marble we have all wrongly assumed filled Ancient Greece.

Since its days as the treasury of Athens and dedication to Athena, the Parthenon has been used as a Christian church, converted into a Turkish mosque complete with minaret, and was even used as a gunpowder store in the seventeenth century – the result of which is its damaged half side and missing roof.

Knowing Your Columns

If you know just one fact about Ancient Greek architecture, it is likely to be that the columns of buildings are described with one of three names: Doric, Ionic or Corinthian. But what on earth does that mean, and why were there distinctions?

In simple terms, these architectural styles are trends that originated in different regions of Ancient Greece. There are several features that typify the buildings of each of these three orders, but the most instantly recognizable is how they designed the rising columns that lifted up the porticos and roofs of their constructions. The names refer to different groups of Greeks: the Dorians, who were dotted about largely in the north and east of Greece; the Ionians, who

Doric   *Ionic*   *Corinthian*

Classical Greek architectural styles.

came from what is now the Turkish coast near Izmir; and the Corinthians from mainland Greece not far from Athens.

The Doric order is typified by simple and undecorated columns. The sturdy design can be seen in the Parthenon in Athens. The Ionic order has slightly thinner and fancier columns, with spirals (or volutes) adorning the head of each one. The Corinthian order goes fancier still, with elaborate acanthus leaves, stalks and flowers carved into the column heads. The Doric and Ionic orders emerged around the sixth and fifth centuries BC, and the Corinthian order very shortly afterwards from about 400 BC onwards. More than just the column heads, each order had particular dimension ratios between column width and height, column placement, and building height, each offering a slightly different feel to the finished construction.

The Greek Theatre

Greek theatres were at the very heart of Ancient Greek culture. Typically a semicircular bowl shape, they are not to be confused with amphitheatres, which go all the way round like the Colosseum in Rome. To help with the construction of the towering tiered seating, Greek theatres were carved into the sides of hills. This meant that some of the most spectacular sites were able to seat up to twenty thousand audience members in one go, each one of whom had an uninterrupted view of the action. There were no 'restricted view' tickets in these venues.

The Great Theatre at Ephesus, Turkey, was first constructed around 250 BC and is a fine example of a Greek theatre. It has a capacity of 25,000 seats.

The acoustic design of these ancient sites is extraordinary to experience. The shape of the tiered seating meant that everyone could hear what was being said on stage, regardless of where they sat. If you visit one of the larger theatres that still stand today, you can climb to the very last row of seats and ask someone to speak from the stage. When they stand in the very centre of the stage facing forwards, they only need to speak in a normal voice for you to hear them from high up in the audience as though they are just a few metres from you.

What we might call the stage was in fact a circular space known as the *orchestra*. From the Greek word meaning 'to dance', the *orchestra* would have included performances from the singing and dancing chorus as part of the plays that were performed. Behind the *orchestra* is the *skena*, the backdrop that typically had architectural features like doors and gates that could easily double up as a number of locations within a play's story. This is where we get the English word 'scene'.

Aside from costumes and simple props, one method of bringing some special effects to performances came in the form of a crane. This allowed actors who played gods to come hovering over the *skena* and be lowered down into the action from the heavens. Often used in Greek tragedy as well as in some comedies, this was a technique to wrap up some more complex stories. The god would appear from the heavens, explain the outcomes of the justice meted out to the protagonists, and the play would end. It has given us the Latin phrase *deus ex machina* ('the god from a machine'), translated from the original Greek phrase, which now refers to stories, movies or situations that come to an abrupt and neatly concluded close.

The Colossus of Rhodes

Ancient Greek writers talked about the Seven Wonders of the World from the second century BC onwards. As trade, travel and war carried Greeks all over the Mediterranean, the Middle East and Asia, they were aware of the amazing civilizations that dotted the known world. The list of the awe-inspiring sites of the ancient world included the Great Pyramid of Giza, the Lighthouse of Alexandria, the Hanging Gardens of Babylon and the Colossus of Rhodes.

The island of Rhodes had been under siege for a year by Demetrius I of Macedon in 304 BC. When Rhodes made an alliance with Ptolemy I of Egypt, an influx of Egyptian soldiers forced the Macedonians to make a hasty retreat, abandoning even their weapons and equipment. The Rhodians sold off all the metal and accessories of war, and built a huge statue of the sun god Helios to commemorate their victory. Forged in bronze, reinforced with iron and filled with stones to weigh it down, the statue rose over 30 metres (nearly 100 feet) above the harbour walls. Some later depictions imagine the sun god straddling the harbour, with one foot either side of the entrance and boats sailing between his legs, but this is deemed to have been technologically unfeasible at the time of its construction.

The Colossus of Rhodes was about the same size as the Statue of Liberty from feet to head, and the New York icon even makes a reference to this Greek statue. At the entrance to her pedestal is inscribed a sonnet called *The New Colossus*, in which the Statue of Liberty is described as being 'Not like the brazen giant of Greek fame, With conquering limbs astride from land to land'.

Construction of the statue was completed in 280 BC, but just fifty-four years later, a powerful earthquake destroyed much of the harbour, and the statue broke at the knees and fell to the ground. It lay there for over eight hundred years and became a famous site in its own right, until it

The Colossus of Rhodes, built to commemorate a monumental victory.

was finally dismantled and sold off as scrap metal by Arab invaders in AD 654.

Greek Pottery

When you think of Ancient Greek pottery, you likely have a familiar image of a two-handled vase, with 2D orange figures depicting a mythological scene (or something more obscene) against a black background. But with so many examples of this style of pottery about, you may wonder why it was the Greeks' format of choice for their art. There are two answers to that question. Firstly, other forms of art are simply much less likely to survive. Some ancient homes, like those on the Greek island Delos, still have intricate floor mosaics that you can see, and only in the Roman cities Pompeii or nearby Herculaneum can you appreciate the richness and variety of painted murals of entire populations frozen in time by the eruption of Mount Vesuvius. Outside of those examples, fired clay pots are much more hardwearing against the disintegration of time.

Greek amphorae containing wine or oil, for example, were transported in this way on boats to other countries.

The second reason that there seems to be so much Greek pottery about is because of the role that vases and vessels had in Ancient Greek society, which shouldn't be underestimated. Vessels allow you to store oil, transport water, pour a cup of wine, trade grains, buy and sell perfume. Of course, unembellished clay amphoras would have been used for large-scale trade, transportation and storage, but the intricacy of the art that is found on so many other examples shows just how important smaller vessels were to daily life in the home.

There are three distinct eras of Greek pottery, each with its own trends and characteristics that reflect what was going on in the Greek world at the time. When viewed as a whole, the different eras show the evolution of artistic ability. The earliest examples from 1000 to 700 BC follow the Geometric style, with vases covered in elaborate geometric patterns and shapes. It is only the later examples from this era that start to show people and animals from mythological scenes, but even they are simple, geometric silhouettes, rather than the detailed images of later eras.

The next distinct style emerged around 700 BC in Corinth. The geometric patterns gave way to influences from Greece's trading routes into Africa and Asia, with curved patterns and the introduction of animals such as the lion, and mythological creatures like the Sphinx, the multiheaded Chimera and the Gorgon.

From about 630 BC, the Athenian style overtook the Corinthian in its quality and artistic skill. Moving to depict more narrative scenes of Greece's rich mythology, the vases typically showed detailed black figures against an orange background. This evolved into Red-figure pottery from 530 BC, where the people were depicted in orange against a black background. This allowed for much more realistic and detailed characterization of facial expressions, flowing cloth and scene elements. It was only with the improving skill of decorators in this era that figures started being shown in poses other than profile, and artistic methods of perspective and layering characters behind one another became possible. This opened the doors to ever more intricate scenes.

Like all art, however, this style of Greek pottery was a trend. The love of it started to wane and by about 320 BC, it had all but disappeared completely.

Recognizing Your Statues

Many examples of statues from the Ancient Greek world exist as decoration to celebrate the human form and the artistic skill of the sculptor. They depict beautiful young girls or boys, athletic discus throwers or unknown warriors showing off their muscles. Many were painted in vivid colours, rather than the white marble we assume them to have been, and show evidence of white or silver eyes and teeth to make them all the more realistic.

Some statues exist to tell a story, to commemorate a powerful myth or to pay homage to the pantheon of gods. The legends we know as Ancient Greek mythology would have been well known to your average Greek – they were the Netflix of the day – and some sculptures are instantly recognizable scenes from iconic stories. When capturing the countless gods, goddesses, heroes and mythological characters in stone, sculptors and artists incorporated visual clues that helped passers-by identify whose image stood before them. Here's your cheat sheet for when you're wandering through Greek or Roman ruins.

CHARACTER	TYPICAL IDENTIFIERS
Apollo	Holds a lyre to show his link to music, or a bow.
Artemis	The goddess of the hunt often holds a bow and quiver, and is depicted with a variety of wild animals. One image has her covered in what are assumed to be bulls' testicles for her links to fertility.
Athena	The goddess of wisdom is often shown with a wise owl, or wearing armour or a shield embellished with Medusa's head. This is for her part in helping Perseus defeat the monster.
Dionysus	The god of wine holds up a bunch of grapes and a full goblet.
Hercules	This hero almost always is wearing the skin of a lion and/or carrying the large club that he used to kill the creature.
Hermes	The messenger god has a winged helmet and winged sandals. If the statue is holding up the severed head of Medusa, it is Perseus, who borrowed Hermes' handy wings for the job.

Medusa	Despite later depictions of this snake-haired gorgon, early artists are more likely to show her with wings and sometimes tusks. Others show her as a beautiful woman.
Poseidon	The god of the sea carries a large trident, with which he stirs up storms. The powerful, frothing waves are often depicted as horses pulling his chariot.
Zeus	The king of the gods often has an eagle by his side – a symbol of power used to this day. He carries a lightning bolt, ready to punish anyone who dares to misstep.

Roman Art and Architecture

The Golden House

A huge area of central Rome was destroyed in a fire in AD 64. Emperor Nero seized the opportunity to extend his residence out onto the land, building a vast palace and grounds on the site. The ostentatious construction contained several buildings, a lake, canals and vineyards, and became known as *Domus Aurea*: the Golden House.

One of the many banqueting halls is described as having a round, rotating ceiling that moved day and night to mimic the heavens, a mechanism likely to have been powered by water from an aqueduct. Other dining rooms had ceilings decorated with carved ivory panels, which could turn and sprinkle guests with falling petals, or reveal pipes that sprayed diners with perfume. Some bathrooms offered fresh water, while others had the option of sulphur-rich spa water. The whole complex was adorned with marble, precious stones, carvings and murals by the wonderfully named artist Fabullus. As well as being the ultimate display of wealth and superiority, the construction of the whole complex would have tested the limits of architectural possibility at that time.

Nero's final statement of power was made in the 30-metre (around 100-foot) bronze statue of himself that stood at one entrance to the palace, known as the Colossus of Nero. Unfortunately for the emperor, he died in AD 68 and all construction on his ill-conceived Golden House ceased. The site was stripped of its valuable materials within a matter of years, while the Colossus had its head replaced and was remodelled as the sun god Sol, and the buildings were eventually filled with earth to be used as foundations for further construction. Nero's chaotic leadership was followed by the Year of Four Emperors, and when the Flavian Dynasty took power the following year, Nero's legacy was subjected to a *damnatio memoriae* – erasing the memory of his existence. The extravagant site was symbolically replaced by something for the people of Rome: the mighty Colosseum, likely named so in defiance of the Colossus that had stood in that place.

The Golden House was only rediscovered in the late fifteenth century, when a happy accident saw a young man fall through a hole in the side of the Esquiline Hill and find himself in an ancient hall surrounded by astonishing murals. It became a cult destination for the artists, libertines and rebels of the Renaissance, lowering themselves on ropes into the cavernous, buried palace to witness first-hand the splendour of the Romans. The Marquis de Sade graffitied his signature down there, as did Casanova. Artists Michelangelo and Raphael were heavily influenced by what they saw, bringing the creativity of Roman artist Fabullus into the most famous paintings and murals of the Renaissance. This is the reason for such a resurgence in classical imagery throughout the Renaissance period across Europe.

The Colosseum

One of Rome's most iconic sites that still stands at one end of the Forum is the Colosseum. The vast amphitheatre for sporting events may have held as many as eighty thousand audience members. Although it was built in AD 80, this capacity would put it in line with the very biggest Olympic arenas that have been built in the modern day. For comparison, London's O2 Arena and New York's Madison Square Garden just about hold 20,000 people each. A series of huge awnings hung over the arena's open roof, bringing some shade to the crowd as well as guiding in a cooling breeze. As you enter one of the Colosseum's eighty entrances today with a throng of tourists, you can't help but hear the clamour of its ancient visitors, pouring in for a day of gladiatorial fights.

The emperor Vespasian was the first of the Flavian Dynasty. He had no right by lineage to rule Rome, so he needed to make a bold statement to the people of the empire. What better way to curry favour than to knock down Nero's ostentatious Golden House and build in its place a mighty arena for the people? Vespasian died before the completion of the building, which was later opened with great fanfare by his son and successor, Titus, who announced 100 days of games in what would have been an unparalleled festival for the city.

A visit to the Colosseum was a full day out for the family. Old bits of pottery acted as tickets, numbered with the section and row of your seat. A hierarchical class system placed the rich and powerful 'courtside', with the seats getting cheaper and less desirable the further you went up the arena's steep sides. The morning would feature a series of animal fights, with some of the most exotic and ferocious beasts from across the Mediterranean and Africa goaded to fight for their lives. Then would come the public executions of criminals, slaughtered in a variety of inventive and gruesome ways, from crucifixion to being mauled by animals. One particularly barbaric game would see two criminals take to the arena floor, one with a sword and the other left to vainly attempt to escape. When one of them emerged victorious, a new criminal would be brought out, handed the one sword, and the hideous game would start over. It was not unheard of for some criminals to commit suicide to end the unfathomable public torture they were facing.

All of this was followed by the main event: the big gladiatorial fights. The gladiators were made up of enslaved people from the growing borders of the empire, together with Roman citizens voluntarily taking up the sport. There was big money in the games, and the most successful gladiators were huge celebrities in their own right, with evidence of ancient merchandise being sold for some of the fighters. Ultimately, however, these men were genuinely fighting for their survival. Slaves could be rewarded with freedom for them and their families, while Roman citizens could win fame, glory and unspeakable wealth.

It is said that Titus' opening games saw the slaughter of 9,000 animals. All that death and blood was soaked up by the sand-covered floor known in Latin as the *harenas* ('the sands'), from where we get the English word 'arena'. Beneath the stadium floor were three-storey-high tunnels, cells and cages to house the many animals, gladiators and criminals for that day's events. This ingenious construction, known as the *hypogeum* ('the underground'), hid a series of man-powered elevators and ramps that could – at a moment's notice – raise a roaring lion or charging rhinoceros into the centre of the arena floor. Imagine the utter thrill for the 80,000 spectators to see such exotic and ferocious animals suddenly leap into the fight as if from nowhere. Four tunnels led out from the *hypogeum* directly to the various gladiatorial schools dotted around the Colosseum, as well as a special tunnel for the emperor to make an exit without mixing with the riffraff in the streets.

The Roman Forum

The Roman Forum is the centre of the ancient city. It was a busy and crowded area, filled with political buildings, sacred sites, temples, markets, law courts and, at one end, the mighty Colosseum. It would have been the lively hub of the city, and indeed of the entire empire, with its many buildings constructed, renovated and rebuilt over hundreds of years from about 497 BC to AD 312. This is where decisions were made, criminals were convicted, citizens did business, where goods and people were traded, and where celebrity gladiators fought to the death.

The Basilica Aemilia and Basilica Julia dominated the area. The long colonnades and vaulted ceilings of these buildings housed the city's most important courts, along with many shops, and there is even something like a chequers board carved into one marble slab on the pavement outside. The lawyer and politician Cicero published his rather pompous – but entertaining – speeches that were delivered in prosecuting some of the most scandalous crimes in Roman high society here. The English word 'forensic', still used in courts today, simply refers to things that were originally discussed in the Forum. The Basilica buildings were later used as churches when Rome turned to Christianity from AD 380 onwards, from where the name *basilica* came to be used for other large churches across Europe.

A small but notable building in the Forum is the round Temple of Vesta. She was the goddess associated with the fire and hearth of the Roman house, which was the source of the warmth, food and security that the home provided. In dedication to her, a flame burned continuously in the Temple of Vesta, and was thought would herald the end of the Roman people if it were ever extinguished. As such, it was tended day and night by up to six Vestal Virgins, a highly prestigious role given to girls selected in childhood, and a post they held for thirty years each if they could maintain the strict morality expected of them.

Several of Rome's leaders built their own forum to expand on the original site. Caesar, Augustus, Vespasian, Domitian and Nerva each have a forum bearing their name within a stone's throw of the original. Perhaps the most impressive to this day is Trajan's Market, with a towering column and temple dedicated to the emperor, two libraries (one Greek and one Latin), a school and the huge market building that you can still walk through today. Built in AD 112, a road busy with taverns and shops ran straight through Trajan's Market. Extensively renovated over the centuries, it rose to six storeys of semicircular arcades that housed shops, taverns, offices and apartments. Free grain was distributed to citizens on the ground floor, and the sixth floor was home to ponds full of fish, thanks to an aqueduct bringing in fresh, flowing water. The whole thing was built on solid marble floors and covered in vaulted concrete ceilings, creating what is the oldest shopping mall in the world.

The Pantheon

You can barely turn a corner in Rome without happening upon another ancient building that is still standing after two millennia, and one of the most unusual and quietly impressive examples is the Pantheon. As you pass through the columns of the portico, you approach two vast bronze doors towering 7.5 metres (almost 25 feet) above you. These are the original doors, so beautifully constructed and balanced that – even today – one person can push them open with little effort. The same lock mechanism is still in use nearly two thousand years later, making this possibly the oldest in the world. Just don't lose the key!

Once inside, you're greeted by one of the most extraordinary sights in Rome: a perfectly spherical dome extends 43 metres (141 feet) in all directions, and in its very top is the *oculus*, an 8-metre (26-foot) hole open to the heavens. It is the only source of light other than through the grand doors, and during a sunny day, a huge column of sunlight moves around the inside of the temple like a reverse sundial. On a wet day, rain cascades down into the centre of the marble floor and disappears through discreet drain holes. In modern-day Rome, the Christian holiday of Pentecost is celebrated with the breathtaking sight of thousands of red rose petals flickering down to the ground – bravely sprinkled over the edges of the *oculus* by some of the city's firefighters, clinging to the rim of the dome's hole.

What makes the Pantheon even more captivating is that its roof remains – to this day – the largest unreinforced concrete dome in the world. Built in 27 BC, the building has had several revamps, but the construction of the most extraordinary dome has baffled architects and engineers for centuries.

Pompeii

There are few sites of the ancient world that are as utterly jaw-dropping to see as the city of Pompeii. Situated in the

Bay of Naples, southern Italy, the city lies in the shadows of the towering Mount Vesuvius. In AD 79, the powerful volcano erupted, and for eighteen hours it showered down pumice stones across the whole region, formed from frothing, bubbling lava hardening into lightweight rocks as they flew tens of kilometres into the air. Pompeii and other towns found their streets, homes and entire existence buried in 3 metres (almost 10 feet) of the rocks across that first day of the eruption, the weight of the stones causing some roofs to collapse. Most of the city's inhabitants fled during this onslaught, but a few stubborn citizens remained. What they encountered on the second day of the eruption was far worse.

A man named Pliny the Younger was caught up in the catastrophe at the age of just eighteen, and his letters giving his harrowing eyewitness account remain a hugely important part of modern volcanology. As Pliny fled to the sea and sailed with other refugees across the vast Bay of Naples, he describes the scene. Vesuvius was pumping gas, thick ash and pumice stones up to 33 kilometres (over 20 miles) into the atmosphere. This dark column of unimaginable vastness dwarfed the mountain and the land beneath it, covered the region in darkness, and even formed its own weather patterns of lightning and rain. The entire bay was covered in floating pumice stone, creating an extraordinary, rocky sea unlike anything they had seen before.

On the second day, the gigantic plume started to buckle under its own weight. Hundreds of millions of tonnes of burning ash, molten rock and searing gases collapsed down from the stratosphere and tore down the sides of the volcano at a speed of 200 metres (656 feet) per second in a series of waves as hot as 360 °C. The city, already under 3 metres of pumice rock, was in a split second encased in a further 3 metres of fine, superheated ash.

The speed and intense heat of these pyroclastic flows gives us a uniquely preserved ancient city. Every man, woman, child, dog and horse that was in the city was incinerated in an instant. By carefully making casts of the cavities they left in the tightly packed ash, we have over one thousand haunting statues showing their very last moments as they leapt to protect themselves from the cloud they saw coming. You can witness squirming dogs, families huddled together, and panicked escapees at the seafront who never made it onto a boat in time.

On a lighter note, what's left of the city itself is nothing short of breathtaking. You can spend a whole day or more wandering the streets of an entire metropolis. Intact homes, takeaway restaurants, bakeries, a brothel, vivid murals, anarchic graffiti, public toilets, bathhouses, markets and theatres are all there along the countless streets and pathways. Never has an ancient civilization been preserved with such purity, where new discoveries are being made by archaeologists every year. And wherever you walk through the city, the dominating silhouette of smoking Mount Vesuvius looms in the background to remind you of its awesome, destructive power.

CHAPTER 8

SCIENCE AND
INVENTIONS

Greek Science and Inventions

Telecommunications

M any inventions of the classical world will astound you equally for their ingenuity as for their relatability to modern life. The first telecommunications device is described in the fourth century BC by Aeneas Tacticus. He was a Greek writer on the strategies of war, and he describes how the Greek armies were able to communicate messages across vast distances almost instantly.

The hydraulic telegraph was made up of two identical containers. They were positioned on key vantage points of neighbouring hills and were filled with the same volume of water. In the water of each container was floated a disc of cork, which had a vertical rod attached to it. The vertical rod poked out of the top of the containers, and would move down as water was emptied from them. The telecommunication came from the fact that the rods had specific messages inscribed into them at certain intervals, such as 'Enemy on sight', 'Cavalry attack' and 'We need wheat'.

A messenger on one hill would raise his flaming torch to signal a message was about to be transmitted.

The messenger on the second hill would raise his torch to indicate he was ready to receive the message. Upon lowering the torches, both messengers would open the tap on their own water container. Because everything had the same dimensions, the water would flow at the same rate, and the rods with their messages inscribed would lower at the same speed.

The messenger on the first hill would raise his torch again when it was time for both soldiers to turn off their taps. Whatever message inscribed on the rod was in line with the top of the container was the bulletin to communicate further. This semaphore system was a huge advance in human communications, and was later adopted by the Romans to send messages as far as from Sicily to Carthage in Tunisia during the First Punic War.

Alarm Clock

A particularly inventive mathematician called Ctesibius is credited with devising the first alarm clock as early as the third century BC. Based in Alexandria, Egypt, which was ruled by the Greeks at the time, Ctesibius was already showing promise as a young barber. In that role, he engineered a counterweight mirror, suspended by a rope that travelled along the ceiling to the corner of the room. There, it was weighted by a lead ball weighing the same as the mirror, meaning the mirror could be moved around at ease by the coiffeurs and would remain in position.

As the lead ball moved up and down in an encasing tube, it let out an interesting whistling sound. This brought about Ctesibius' next invention: the water organ, the precursor to the church instrument used today. The tireless innovator soon turned his focus to the water clock. Already around for millennia before him, water clocks trickled water from one bucket into another, and the passage of time could be noted by the amount of water that had passed through. This design was used in Greek and Roman courtrooms and brothels alike to keep things on schedule.

Ctesibius' several innovations on this ancient design saw him float pointers on the water to indicate on a scale a clear period of time that had passed. One version floated a piston on the water that was attached to a cog on a dial, giving us the very first mechanical clock face. Another version

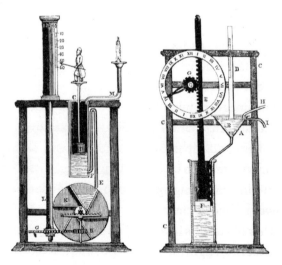

An engraving depicting Greek water clocks.

included multiple chambers to limit the apparent slowing down of time that came with more rudimentary bucket designs as the water emptied. A more accurate clock was not invented for another 1,800 years.

Perhaps the most impressive innovation was to design a series of mechanical movements that would happen when the water reached a particular level. In this way, Ctesibius invented the first alarm clocks that would blow trumpets, drop a pebble on a gong, or make bird statues sing at a designated time.

Automatic Doors

Another Alexandrian man was inspired by the many engineering feats of Ctesibius. In the first century AD, Heron of Alexandria became obsessed with the mechanical possibilities that came from moving water, shifting air and creating vacuums. Many of his inventions were toys, amusement pieces or designed to create a sense of drama and divine magic in temples. One such marvel is known as Heron's fountain, a small contraption made from a series of chambers and pipes that create a handheld fountain that spurts water into its own filling tank. In this way, the fountain can keep going for several minutes purely through the power of hydraulics.

Another of Heron's inventions was automatic doors. His design describes lighting a fire on an altar, which expands the air in hidden tubes and chambers beneath the altar.

The pressure pushes water into a bucket concealed under the temple floor, which in turn is attached by pulleys to the double doors of the temple. The doors fly open as if by the divine magic of prayer. Extinguishing the fire allows the water to flow back to its original place, and the doors close again.

Heron's inventions were truly remarkable for the age. Employing similar techniques, they included statues that were made to pour wine libations onto an altar when a fire was lit, and all manners of singing birds, trumpets and hissing snake statues – all brought to life by hidden pipes, pulleys, levers and vacuums that were activated by something as simple as lighting a fire or pouring on water.

ROMAN SCIENCE AND INVENTIONS

Watermill

In Barbegal in the south of France are the ruins of an extraordinary technological advancement from the second century AD. Cascading down one side of a valley is a series of buildings, which housed a total of sixteen watermills. Water was fed via an aqueduct to the lip of the valley, from where it flowed down eight graduated steps, each with two watermills side by side.

Water turned the wheel of each mill, and poured down onto the next step below, creating what is considered the first industrial complex in European history. The construction was engineered to maximize the flow of water onto each wheel, offering highly efficient machinery that worked with no human or animal energy required. Roman mills were used to grind flour, process building materials, and to provide the power to cut stone and wood on an industrial scale. It is thought that the watermills at Barbegal could have processed enough flour to feed at least ten thousand people every day.

It feels almost audacious to refer to the Industrial

The Barbegal watermill, Fontvieille, France.

Revolution that took place with the watermills of Great Britain from 1760 onwards, when the Romans had their very own version some 1,600 years beforehand.

Roman Roads

The success of the Roman civilization relied on its ability to move about its own territory with ease. Roman roads opened up the ability to trade around the whole Mediterranean and beyond. They allowed messages, stories, technology and goods to reach every corner of the Roman world. Most importantly, they enabled the fearsome Roman armies to reach and conquer new territories.

The first major road was the Via Appia that extended over 570 kilometres (about 350 miles) south-east from Rome down to the town of Tarentum, and eventually to Brindisium on the Adriatic coast. Both were important strategic positions for Rome, not least as trading ports to Greece and Tunisia. Parts of the Via Appia are still in use today in Rome, and you can explore ancient parts of the road by foot. In all, the Romans would go on to construct 80,000 kilometres (nearly 50,000 miles) of roads, from modern-day Britain to Iraq, from Germany to Tunisia. Typified by long, straight construction, with sloped edges for easy drainage, and solid foundations, many Roman roads are still in use today, including some that have become highways that traverse Europe.

In the ruins of Pompeii, just outside Naples in Italy, you can wander through the Roman streets of the ancient city. The eruption of Mount Vesuvius in AD 79 covered the city in layers of pumice and ash, preserving it in remarkable condition to explore today. You see not only the roads, but the pedestrian crossings at each major junction. Large slabs act as stepping stones from one side of the street to the other, keeping Roman pedestrians above the drainage water, sewage and horse manure that would have poured down the streets. The stone slabs are a precise distance from one another to allow the wheels of a cart to roll through unobstructed.

Roman Baths

Public bathhouses, or *thermae*, were a focal point of Roman society. It wasn't just about having a bath; it was the equivalent of a spa day out, where citizens met, socialized and did business. Other than in a few unseemly locations, men and women bathed separately, and were treated to a series of spa experiences. In the grander *thermae*, men had space for exercise in the *gymnasium*. The English word 'gym' comes via the Romans, but is originally from the Greek word *gymnos*, meaning naked. This is how exercise was done in the classical world.

After a spot of naked exercise, they would sweat it off in a hot room, indulge in a steam room and recover in a cold room. Large bathing pools were heated by fires, hot air and smoke that was channelled through hollow walls that encased the water. The surfaces would sometimes get so hot that bathers needed to wear special shoes to protect their feet from the heat. Olive oil was liberally applied to the skin, and eventually scraped off, alongside the sweat and water, with a curved metal blade known as a *strigilis*.

The ruins of baths that have survived indicate luxurious surroundings, with marble floors, intricate mosaics and elaborate reliefs and statues. The *thermae* were the original gentlemen's club, where Rome's citizens would spend the day of leisure and business. The Latin word for business is *negotium*, which means 'not leisure' and gives us the English word 'negotiation'. It is in these baths where – at leisure – important deals and business relationships were formed.

Roman Aqueducts

The rapid growth of the Roman civilization brought with it an unparalleled demand for water. Not only was this essential for sustaining and washing the huge populations of Rome and beyond, but also for agriculture to feed them, for the huge population of cattle and horses that supported them, for the public baths, sewage systems and private fountains. Water from aqueducts powered industrial endeavours like the watermills at Barbegal (see page 209), and is even said to have filled amphitheatres like the Colosseum with water for staged sea battles.

Originally a technology to sustain the ballooning population of the city of Rome, remnants of aqueducts are found throughout the Roman Empire on all sides of the Mediterranean. The longest stretch is over 240

A classic example of a Roman aqueduct, Pont del Diable (Devil's Bridge), Catalonia, Spain.

kilometres (more than 150 miles) used to supply the city of Constantinople – modern-day Istanbul in Turkey.

The water in Roman aqueducts was moved entirely by gravity, so the channels, ditches and iconic arched elevations all had to be constructed at specific inclines across vast distances. Too steep, and the water would gush out at every junction and cause irreparable erosion to the whole construction. Too gradual, and the water would evaporate and the channel silt up. Roman architects recommended an incline equivalent to just 1 metre (3.28 feet) across 4,800 metres (about 3 miles). The engineering feat of achieving this when contending with hills, valleys and huge distances should not be underestimated.

When faced with a valley gap too large to bridge over, the water was fed into a holding tank on one ridge. From there, it was sent through a series of lead pipes down the steep sides, across the valley floor, up the escarpment on the other side of the valley and into a receiving tank. In positioning the receiving tank at a lower altitude than the holding tank, and by constructing absolutely airtight lead pipes, the system acted as a siphon that constantly sucked water up the steep valley sides.

It is a testament to the ingenuity of Roman engineers that some of their ancient aqueducts are still in use today. Rome's famous Trevi Fountain is still supplied by the Aqua Virgo aqueduct that was constructed in 19 BC. Their ability to harness water across the Mediterranean really made the Empire the superpower that it was.

Concrete

Concrete was not a Roman invention, but they improved upon the earlier composites that had been used by the Greeks, developing a paste that was easy to store and that would harden when water was added. The ease of use revolutionized the Roman architectural boom from the third century BC onwards. Suddenly, they weren't constrained by traditional brick and stone masonry, and could imagine and create entirely new methods of construction. They even perfected a concrete that would harden underwater, transforming the construction of ports, bridges and aqueducts.

There are several notable concrete constructions that are still standing today. The Pantheon in Rome boasts the largest unreinforced concrete dome in the world – it has not been bettered since it was built in 27 BC. The Colosseum's stunning construction in about AD 80 was largely with concrete, and the six-storey shopping mall of Trajan's Market built in AD 100 was covered with a vast vaulted concrete ceiling.

Studies of Roman concrete have established that it is just as strong as the mixes we use today, save for the reinforcement of steel rods used in modern construction.

Takeaway Food

When Mount Vesuvius erupted in AD 79, pyroclastic flows instantly buried the towns of Pompeii and Herculaneum, preserving Roman life in a moment in time, unlike any other site of the ancient world. New discoveries are being made by archaeologists all the time, who are lucky enough to be given a plot and tasked with seeing what they can uncover. It is believed that one-third of Pompeii and up to three-quarters of Herculaneum remain unexcavated.

A recent discovery was a particularly well preserved takeaway shop, one of about eighty to have been available to busy workers in the city. It is clear that food on the go wasn't just a fad; it was a major part of daily life in Pompeii. The concrete counter is beautifully painted with images of chickens and ducks – perhaps a visual menu of what was available. The inlaid bowls on the counter contained traces of duck, goat, beef, pork, fish and snails.

It is utterly breathtaking that we can see not just a snapshot of Roman life, but that we can literally see what they were eating on the day that the eruption destroyed the city.

EPILOGUE:
THE CLASSICAL WORLD
LIVES ON

The classical world isn't just a relic of the past. The Ancient Greeks and Romans are not just an influence on our modern-day existence – they have shaped it entirely. The richness of their lives is present in the structure of our courtrooms, in the design of our sporting arenas, in the stories told in Hollywood, in the mathematics, astronomy and philosophy we study, and in the very words we speak.

We continue to be connected to the classical world by the human experiences we share. The vividness of the emotions captured by the heartache of their tragedies and by the heartbreak of their star-crossed lovers can elicit the same feelings in us today as it did for audiences over 2,500 years ago. We delight at the story of the Cyclops. We are gripped by the battles at Troy, and we are left hollow by the lovers separated by death.

So, let your history books gather dust on the shelf. Instead, cry at the downfall of Oedipus, be astounded by a walk around the Colosseum, and walk up to the takeaway counter in Pompeii just as its citizens did on the day disaster struck. Step into the living, breathing world of the Ancient Greeks and Romans, and you'll realize how our modern lives are simply another chapter in the ongoing narrative that began in the Classical World.

ACKNOWLEDGEMENTS

I extend my heartfelt gratitude to the entire team at Michael O'Mara Books for their tireless efforts in bringing this book to life. Special thanks go to Gabriella Nemeth for keeping the ship on course; to David Inglesfield for copy-editing with utter dedication to the detail; to David Woodroffe and Aubrey Smith for their detailed maps and illustrations that help bring the ancient world to life; and to Jessica Benhar for the wonderful cover.

Select Bibliography
and Further Reading

Homer, *The Odyssey*, trans. Robert Fagles (Penguin, 1990)

Virgil, *The Aeneid*, trans. Robert Fagles (Penguin, 2010)

Homer, *The Odyssey*, trans. Emily Wilson (WW Norton & Company, 2018)

Homer, *The Iliad*, trans. Emily Wilson (WW Norton & Company, 2023)

Harris, Robert, *Pompeii* (Arrow, 2009)

Fry, Stephen, *Mythos: The Greek Myths Retold* (Penguin, 2018)

Beard, Mary, *Emperor of Rome* (Profile Books, 2023)

Gaardner, Jostein, *Sophie's World*, trans Paulette Møller (Phoenix, 1995)

Plato, *The Republic*, trans. Desmond Lee (Penguin, 1974)

Hero, *The Pneumatics of Hero of Alexandria*, trans. and ed. Bennet Woodcroft (Taylor Walton and Maberly, 1851)

Trypanis, Constantine A. (ed.), *The Penguin Book of Greek Verse* (Penguin, 1971)

Chadwick, John, *The Mycenaean World* (Cambridge University Press, 1976)

Jones, Peter and Sidwell, Keith (eds), *The World of Rome* (Cambridge University Press, 1997)

Picture Credits

The publisher would like to thank the following sources for their kind permission to reproduce the pictures in this book:

Page 14: The Greek gods and goddesses family tree. Illustration by David Woodroffe

Page 22: Eros, the god of love statue. Photo Sampajano_Anizza/Shutterstock

Page 23: Cronus abducting one of his children. Photo Public Domain

Page 26: Atlas in front of the Rockefeller Center, NYC. Photo Kamira/Shutterstock

Page 46: Bronze statue of Hermes. Photo Granger/Bridgeman Images

Page 49: Cylix of Apollo bowl. Photo ZDE via Wikimedia Commons

Page 57: Commodus styled as Hercules statue. Photo Sacred Spark Art/Shutterstock

Page 72: Achilles bandaging Patroclus cup. Photo Public Domain

Page 75: Statue of Romulus and Remus with the Capitoline Wolf. Photo MisterStock/Shutterstock

Page 80: Empire of Alexander the Great. Map by David Woodroffe

Page 93: *The Death of Julius Caesar.* Photo Public Domain

Page 103: Emperor Nero's bust. Photo Alexander Sviridov/Shutterstock

Page 109: Roman Colosseum illustration. Photo © NPL – DeA Picture Library/Bridgeman Images

Page 114: Trojan Horse. Illustration by Aubrey Smith

Page 124: Hannibal's route from Hispania through the Alps. Map by David Woodroffe

Page 139: Socrates bust. Photo Osama Shukir Muhammed Amin FRCP(Glasg) via Wikimedia Commons

Page 155: Odysseus and the Sirens on red vase. Photo Public Domain

Page 159: *Dido building Carthage.* Photo Public Domain

Page 176: Orpheus and Eurydice mosaic. Photo Gre regiment via Wikimedia Commons

Page 182: Classical Greek architectural styles. Photo North Wind Picture Archives/Alamy Stock Photo

Page 184: Ephesus Ancient City theatre aerial view. Photo RauL C7/Shutterstock

Page 187: Colossus of Rhodes. Photo Public Domain

Page 188: Greek amphorae. Photo Ad Meskens via Wikimedia Commons

Page 206: Engraving depicting Greek water clocks. Photo World History Archive/Alamy Stock Photo

Page 210: Barbegal Water Mill. Photo Classic Image/Alamy Stock Photo

Page 213: Pont del Diable aqueduct. Photo Karel Gallas/Shutterstock

Every effort has been made to acknowledge correctly and contact the source and/or copyright holder of each picture and the publisher apologizes for any unintentional errors or omissions, which will be corrected in future editions of this book.

INDEX

Page numbers in bold refer to images